THE
HORSEY
LIFE

THE
HORSEY
LIFE

**A journey of discovery with
a rather remarkable mare**

SIMON BARNES

This paperback edition published in 2010

First published in 2008 by
Short Books
3A Exmouth House
Pine Street, London EC1R 0JH

A CIP catalogue record for this book
is available from the British Library.

ISBN 978-1-906021-94-8

Printed in the UK by CPI Bookmarque, Croydon, CR0 4TD

To all the horsey ladies in my life...
especially the one I married

First sight

I don't want to start on the wrong foot, so let's not talk about love at first sight, or any guff like that. Besides, it didn't happen at first sight, and anyway, it wasn't love. But in that first couple of hours of our lives together – and we have been together for all but twenty years – there was certainly something. There was a connection. Was it entirely one way?

Well, let's worry about that later. All I can say is that there was something. Her name was Dolly, and I thought it was a stupid name right from the first, and I've hardly ever used it since. It suited her not a bit. She was not a My Little Pony sort of a horse, not a dolly-girl, not winsome and winning, not even terribly pretty. A stubby little mare, bright bay with remarkably large ears. A white star on her forehead shaped like Madagascar. A huge arse; which is good, not bad, because that's where the power comes from. Not a horse that would turn heads, no, just a very horse-like horse. She stood, quiet, docile, as I approached her. To tell the truth, I was a bit disappointed not to be offered something more lively. Ha. I placed a foot in the iron and swung on board... and in that single instant the horse came alive.

It was as if I had turned a key. All the lights came on, she started buzzing. Actually, I was a little alarmed: a little intimidated. She was rather more horse than I was expecting.

When you first touch the reins of a horse, there is an instant exchange of information. It flows both ways: now I'm quite certain about that. It's probably true that in the first electric contact, the horse knows more about you than you know about the horse. The horse instantly learns something about your competence, balance, level of fear, whether you like to bully, whether you can be bullied, and perhaps, and most importantly, whether or not you are simpatico. But the rider certainly learns something, if not as much, about the horse, horses being more highly tuned than humans when it comes to picking up small nuances of mood. What I learned in that first moment of contact was that I had something ever so slightly special. Not necessarily special for everybody: but definitely something special for me.

I rode her out with two or three others. The usual thing: a little roadwork, some bridleways, a place or two where you could kick on a bit. And I have a vivid memory of this, a strong physical memory, what psychologists call a psychokinetic memory, of the way the little mare moved. It's a hard thing to explain, because the memory is all in my hands and my arse and my legs. She was so light, but with an altogether unexpected amount of power behind. I knew even then, before I even thought of trying her, that she could jump like a little stag. What I didn't know was that the way she carried herself – light before, weight all behind – would come close to breaking my heart.

She was a handful all right, on that first ride: but she was not wicked, she was fun. That was quite definitely, incontrovertibly a two-way thing: she loved to be out and active and given a licence to express herself. She hated to be fussed. She was looking to explode at any time: always eager to step up a pace, every walk edging towards a trot, every trot seeking to become a canter, every canter on the brink of a gallop. But she wasn't pulling and fighting and straining. And I never even started looking for a fight myself: I found that, almost in spite of myself, I was relaxing, giving her a little more leeway than she was perhaps used to, telling her there was nothing to get tense about, that we would have our fun in due course. I discovered that if I sat back and deep, she would listen, and canter short and neat and clever with quite miraculous balance. It was a bit like driving a fast boat with an outboard engine: all the power behind you, the front end light and sketchy, and the sense of control ditto.

And that's the memory of that first encounter. Not eyes meeting across a crowded room; nothing soppy. Just that connection: the physical memory of it. The exuberance was a shared thing. I really can still feel it: the infinite number of tiny adjustments, a small correction here, a generous relaxation of the reins there, a pat to tell her I was cool and so was she. It was not that there was something between us: it was almost as if there was nothing between us. I was for the most part sitting as deep as I knew how, in close contact, trying to sit as if I had been glued on. And there was a fusion between our two minds: I was tuned into her, I understood something of her. And perhaps I was understood – who knows? So I got off her and resolved to have nothing more to do with her.

Evolutionary master stroke

I remember standing beside the gallops at Arundel Castle, watching a string of racehorses going past. They travelled in groups of three or four, because a mad cavalry charge of all 50 at once would be rather too exciting for all concerned. This was the second lot at John Dunlop's yard, and the two-year-olds were showing us their best stuff. Dunlop, a tall man with a farmer's cracked veins in his cheeks, a tendency to speak in a patrician drawl, in those days a fag permanently on the go, continued his usual recitation of pedigrees and occasional cryptic comments on the talent before him. ("That's a silly horse that tries to run away all the time. But when you let him he doesn't do it terribly fast.")

I was a regular guest at Castle Stables in those days, researching a book about a year in Dunlop's yard. And in my presence, Dunlop occasionally let his mind run free, thinking out loud, perhaps from the novelty of having a Boswell beside him. "I don't think horses can be terribly clever, do you?" he said, eyes looking critically at the action of a particularly well-bred little colt. "You can't be terribly clever if you let people sit on you, can you?" Dunlop taught me many things about sport, racing, horses, life, style, manners, decency and horsemanship. But after long consideration, I have come to the conclusion that in this instance, he was wrong. The horse is a genius.

Consider the facts. There are more than a million horses in Britain alone. Horses are thriving. They breed, they prosper, they increase. All over the world, there are horses. Wherever horses can be kept, people keep horses. It's as if we simply cannot help ourselves. Thanks to *Homo sapiens*, *Equus caballus* is the most fabulous success story.

There are other species in the genus *Equus*, and all bar one is in some kind of trouble. This lone exception is *Equus burchelli*, the plains zebra, which is doing well in national parks across Africa: mainly because people pay good money to go and see them. There are two other zebra species, Grevy's and mountain, both classified as endangered, while the quagga, another zebra species (or subspecies, as some authorities prefer) is extinct. The wild horse, Przewalski's horse, is down to a few hundred, and its status as a true species is now contested, particularly as it has interbred with domestic horses. The African wild ass is critically endangered; the Asian wild ass is vulnerable. The kiang and the onager, regarded by some as separate species, and by others as subspecies of the Asian wild ass, are endangered; the Syrian subspecies is extinct.

But *Equus caballus* prospers where the rest struggle: and the reason is blindingly obvious. It is because horses have adopted the strategy of domestication. They have thrown in their lot with humans; and as a result, they are the dominant equid on the planet. I am not, of course, attributing a conscious choice in all this, perish the thought. Evolution is a vast, complex and enthralling subject: and it is also, at least to a degree, a crap-shoot. The dinosaurs dominated the earth for 100 million years, and the mammals never had a chance. Then the earth bumped into a meteor and the dinosaurs couldn't hack it any more. But the scruffy, insignificant, uninspiring little mammals were able to cling on. And so, by means of dumb luck, the mammals inherited the earth. Humans went on to become the dominant large animals on the planet, with the result that any animal that has what it takes to live with humans has prospered. Rats profit from out rubbish, blue tits from our generosity, dogs from our gregariousness, pigeons from our agriculture, pheasants from our murderousness. And horses profit from – well, from our horsiness. There is a strange link between our two species: and it has worked greatly to the profit of both.

Horses domesticate. They respond well to life in artificial conditions. No doubt it began when humans discovered that having half a ton of meat on your doorstep made for an easier life than going out to hunt. In the millennia that followed, horses became used for burden, for transport, for war, for agriculture, and the horse prospered. But then they invented the internal combustion engine, and horses were no longer necessary. It was logical, then, that the domestic horse would veer towards extinction: perhaps to be kept alive by a few mad enthusiasts, of the kind that lovingly maintain vintage cars.

But it didn't happen. There are as many horses as ever. And this is where the true genius of the horse comes in. Horses first made themselves essential in a wholly utilitarian way. But when their usefulness was over, they changed their strategy. They joined the leisure market. We no longer keep horses because we need to; but we still keep horses. And it can only be because we want to. The horse's evolutionary strategy is an extraordinary affinity for humankind. And here is the question that lies at the heart of it: who's exploiting whom?

Unfair to the horse

I rode her again; we had a ball. It was better, if anything. I knew she was a wild little thing, but I also knew by then that she wasn't crazy. I also knew she was for sale. I had decided to buy a horse. But not that one. She was too good for me.

Cindy, my wife, knows a few things about horses, and a few more things about me. "Do you mean you can't ride her? She's too much for you?" "No, not at all. I mean, I have to be at my best, but that's good. She's great." "You're not scared of her?"

A fair question. Anyone is entitled to be frightened of any horse: anyone can lose his nerve at any time. But I wasn't frightened. I was genuinely excited by the challenges she had for me. Already, she was bringing from me things I didn't know I possessed, and their discovery was enthralling. But I was still determined not to buy her.

"But why not?"

"She could compete at a much higher level than I could ever take her to. It would be a waste." It was a kind of guilt. It is obviously a horseman's duty to bring out the full

15

competitive potential of a horse. Isn't it? I mean, if I only pottered about doing local shows, it would be unfair, wouldn't it? Unfair to the horse, that is.

Cindy kindly made me understand that I was talking shite. "You like her, you can ride her, you can have fun competing with her, you can have fun riding out, you can give her a good life. What's wrong with that?" Not for the first, nor for the last time, Cindy had made me see sense. She started to refer to the horse as Dolly Dolores, one of those jokes that demonstrate the rule that in marriage, there is no such thing as a bad joke. I learned that Dolly was a mere stable name; her pedigree or formal name was even worse – Alive and Kicking. But never mind the names. I had recently received a royalty cheque for the book about Dunlop's yard. So the following day, I made out a cheque myself for £1,500. She was mine.

Or, if you like, I was hers.

A gene for horsiness

Horsiness frequently runs in families. There seems to be a gene for horsiness. Consider my own lot. We were brought up in Streatham, in south London, not great horse-riding country. Neither parent had the remotest sympathy, interest or understanding of horses. We used to ride sometimes in the summer holidays: so I knew how to stay on. I quite liked it, but always believed that it was nothing more than a visit to an alien world. My father had, after all, told me that horsey people were awful, and that "you never see a pretty girl on a horse". I learned later that he must have led a very sheltered life, at least in some respects. With family pressures like this, it was obviously impossible to imagine myself becoming a horsey person. True: my younger sister actually had lessons for a while, but perhaps she begged for them. There was a time when she spent Saturdays at a local riding school helping out, as young girls do, until she grew out of it. And that was that. That was the Barnes family's horsey life.

And now I have four horses, while there are rather

more in my sister's family, which includes three horsey daughters. When I visit them, one niece or another will generally have a horse ready for me; we ride out, and it is a joy for all concerned. But we are banned from talking horse at family get-togethers, because my middle sister and her lot are left out. The gene for horsiness has passed them by, or has not been expressed.

My younger sister and I both got horsey later in life. At first I thought it was one of those rum coincidences, but now I'm not so sure. That is because a picture turned up. I have it on my desk; it shows a young man, sitting on a nice-looking little cob with its tail trimmed ultra-short. The man has sergeant's stripes on his arm. If you look carefully – the print is somewhat faded – you can see a background of tents. This is my grandfather, my mother's father, and he served in the First World War in the Royal Artillery, in Salonika. He had never kept a diary in his life, but did so while he was in the army, for the excellent reason that it was forbidden. He didn't write of his own feelings, or the horses he had dealings with: rather, he jotted down technical details of the guns they fired, at what time, how much, in what direction. Most of it was in exquisite spidery Pitman shorthand: the sparse telegrammic details of a forgotten conflict. When he died, we passed the diaries on to the Imperial War Museum, who were delighted to have these relics from an under-documented campaign. He would have laughed a good deal about the irony of this – the unofficial and wicked becoming the official and the cherished – had he but known.

He told us many tales of his soldiering, but never much about the horses. It wasn't a big thing for him, just a natural and inevitable part of life. His own grandfather was a gamekeeper, his mother had ambitions to escape from the economic constraints of her class and the country life. The local grammar school was in theory open to all, but you had to pass an exam in Latin to get in. And here was the catch: Latin was taught only in the local fee-paying prep school. So this redoubtable lady taught herself Latin and then taught her two boys, with the result that Percy, my grandfather, joined the middle classes, worked as a pioneer in vocational guidance, was a Fabian socialist, passed the plate round in church, went to the cricket at Edgbaston, moved to the green and pleasant Birmingham suburb of King's Heath, and left the country and the horsey life behind. It was to sprout again on our side of the family after skipping a generation.

And I was as surprised as anyone when I learned this: both when I discovered that I had the stuff of horsiness in me, and when I realised that it was also a family thing, a thing I could trace back, a thing I could see stretching forward with my nieces. Where does it come from? Why? No doubt people with an affinity for these big and dangerous animals were pretty useful at most periods of human history, while an exceptional performer in that sphere would be cherished. That goes right back to the dawn of civilisation, and the domestication of animals. I suspect that the horseman was an early specialist in the history of human evolution.

At the same time, horses that lacked the reverse affinity, horses that failed to respond to humankind and to domestication, would simply be discouraged: killed, eaten, not bred from. Only those horses who had an equal and opposite affinity for humans would have been cherished in their turn. It is a symbiosis that has lasted from prehistory through to modern times: horses can't do without humans, but then humans – some humans – really can't do without horses. And I am one of them. It only took me 28 years to find out.

Revelation

There was a steep, not-quite-vertical slope that led from a lower bridleway to an old railway embankment. It was perhaps twenty feet high. She always took this in half a dozen crazy galloping bounds. She would explode out of whatever pace she was in, and shoot up to the top as if she had been fired from a gun. This took a bit of getting used to: it's the sort of thing that can fling a rider "out the back door" as horsey people say. That's an unenviable experience: I had already gone through it a couple of times on other horses.

I had been taught to ride in a strict and serious and proper fashion: and part of the teaching was to make sure I did nothing that would allow the horse to develop bad habits. It was your responsibility to make sure that the horse was eminently suitable for riders other than yourself. You didn't, for example, always canter at the same spot, or the horse would get into the habit of taking off at this point and disconcerting a rider who was not expecting it. Nor did you always stop at the same place, for the same reason. It was your duty to make sure that the horse was suitable for everyone: it was only fair to the others: it was only fair to yourself: it was only fair to the horse.

So I tried a good few times to make her walk up the slope like a nice civilised mare. Never succeeded once. Every time we reached the bottom of the slope, she took a great bite of air and went up the slope as if the dogs were after her. Once at the top, she would settle happily at whatever pace I suggested. I tried holding her tight: she merely blasted straight through the bit. I tried approaching the slope with no contact on the bit whatsoever, the reins long and drooping: she went up the slope in about three strides. I tried – but no matter. She ran up the slope no matter what I tried.

It was then I had a Damascene moment. I thought: what the fuck does it matter?

And so, every time we approached the slope, instead of grabbing at the reins and trying to teach her something, I took a handful of mane. That way, when she exploded, there would be no banging her in the mouth with the bit and no throwing my weight back in the saddle. It became a routine: walk up to slope, grab mane, explode, then adjust to whatever pace seemed suitable for the day.

I felt slightly wicked about this, slightly defiant. But the truth was that it didn't matter, and the reason that it didn't matter was that so far as I was concerned, the habit of explosion represented no surprise, no danger, no problem. I didn't care about anyone else, because no one was ever going to ride that little mare except me. We could do what the fuck we liked. And we did.

Lifewish

The horse is the pet that can kill. It is important to come to terms with this truth. It is not self-dramatising: merely an acceptance of the fact that horses are dangerous, and sometimes lethally so. If you get involved in the horsey life, you are going to get hurt and you regularly find yourself in potentially deadly situations.

Danger is a part of it, but not the point of it. It is not like parachuting, in which the ultimately life-affirming defiance of death is the heart and soul of the sport. I remember talking to a sport parachutist, and I tried to get him to explain what it feels like. He was insistent that it's not about, hey, let's all go up in an aeroplane and defy death. He talked about the exhilaration of a jump, the euphoria on completion, the realisation of "how green the bloody grass is". And the one thing he really insisted on was that he was not remotely attracted by death. He was not interested in death, didn't want to die, had no deathwish whatsoever. He jumped out of aeroplanes because he loved being alive. It was a lifewish, then.

That is how I have always felt about horses. I don't like them because they're dangerous; on the other hand, it would be deluding myself to say that I like them in spite of the fact that they are dangerous. Horses have never been a proving ground for me, a way of testing my courage. Nor have they been a sort of bungee jump, an adrenalin hit. The horses themselves are too demanding of attention. And the more I got involved with Dolores, the more complex the issue of danger became. My feelings, my sensations, my emotions were not the only things on the agenda. There was another to consider.

By the time I bought the little mare, I had already done a lot of competing, including the scary discipline of cross-country. I must point out here that I have only ever competed at a low level, the lowest of the low, and that a more advanced and dangerous level of competition would always have been beyond my ability and my courage. But I had been sent halfmad with the excitement of it all, and was very much looking forward to doing it all over again. I wanted to have some big times, some high times. I wanted to taste the thrill of being out on the edge, galloping a horse at a series of unyielding fences. So I was actively seeking the scarier side of the horsey life, and doing so for the same reason that the parachutist leapt from his aeroplane. But there was a difference: neither the aeroplane nor the silk of the parachute is alive. I was not looking for a vehicle to take me into an area of danger: I was looking for a companion. For a fellow-conspirator.

A pint of Pernod

Like measles or Catholicism, horsiness is best dealt with in early life. In youth, recovery from these things is not only possible, but easy. Many people manage it, but after a critical age, all three of these things are likely to affect the rest of your life. Mid-twenties is no time to contract horsiness. Horsiness is generally reckoned to be something to do with growing up, specifically, with girls growing up. When people ask my why I like horses, I generally tell them it's because I haven't discovered boys yet. You seem to need a fair number of jokes when you come to explaining the horsey life: after all, it's much easier to make a joke than to start trying to explain. But since I have started, I suppose I had better carry on.

It is probably Lucy's fault. There she was: trim, slim and gorgeous, dark eyes and a mouth I badly wanted to kiss, an Indian girl without much of a self-esteem problem, drinking Pernod out of a pint glass. How could I resist? This being the firm's Christmas party, I made a pass at her and missed. Not very original, I admit. I maintain to this day that a kiss was landed; she says that if so, it escaped her notice.

So we became pals instead, and indeed, remain so. And Lucy, at that time, loved riding horses, so we occasionally went to riding stables and rode out, and I always enjoyed it, though I wouldn't have gone without her. Then, one day, we decided to push the boat out, and went for a two-hour ride. We went, poor townies that we were, across Wimbledon Common and into Richmond Park. And the sudden freedom of this was more than intoxicating. It was addicting.

The horses galloped. Not a brisk canter: a flat-out give-it-everything gallop. Flat out is, I suspect, one of the many horsey terms that lie fossilised in our language: the transition from a canter – a bouncy gait in three-four time – to a gallop is a move into something smooth and unbouncy and in a four-four time too rapid to count.

There is a wildness in Richmond Park. It is open and studded with mature trees, rather like the savannah from which we humans originally sprang; and there I was, employing the world's most ancient transport system in an absolute transport of exhilaration. And I still couldn't ride. Not really.

But we kept going back. And then, when our free days no longer coincided, I found myself at one of those splits in the road, and I took the one that leads to full-blown horsiness. I started to ride without Lucy. I started to ride by myself. It really was that good. I didn't have much money, and what I did have I tried to keep for important things like drink and saving up to go and live in Asia. But I still managed to find enough to ride out across the park every fortnight.

There was a moment of revelation. I was riding out with the yard's owner, who, I remember, always rode in sharply creased trousers, and with a narrow-brimmed trilby on his head. I never once saw it shift, no matter how fast we went. He was a neat and accomplished horseman, and when his horse went into a canter, he did something I'd never seen before. He stood up. And I was entranced by the beauty of this. I didn't know you were allowed to stand up, unless you were a jockey.

There was just the two of us on this ride, and so I tucked behind him, so he couldn't see what I was doing, and when we next cantered, I too stood up. The effect was to throw my balance forward over the horse's withers – not that I knew what a wither was, but I can tell you now that it's the highest bit along the back, the point of the, as it were, shoulders. My knees slid comfortably into the roll of the saddle, not that I knew saddles had rolls. And instead of feeling as if I was sitting on a small earthquake, I was rising above the turmoil, using my balance, and finding my hands much freer. I didn't need the reins to hold on with any more, to the great relief, no doubt, of the horse. It was a moment of freedom. Suddenly I was riding.

I wanted more.

Alone at last

I have done an awful lot of things on and with horses. I have competed in showjumping, dressage, cross-country, eventing; I have done some endurance riding, and have ridden world and European champions in this sport; I have ridden a Grand Prix dressage horse; I have reschooled a racehorse into an eventer; I have ridden western style and performed spins and crash-halts without a bridle; I have played polo; I have done a four-day trek; I have ridden out with a string of racehorses on Newmarket Heath. But the best thing I have ever done with a horse is to hack out by myself.

That is to say, to ride around the countryside in the company of nobody except a horse. My horse. I had been introduced to this pleasure when I got involved with horses during the four years I lived in Asia. Now I was doing it again, but better, in the company of my new-bought and joyful little mare.

I remember the first ride we took together alone. I had written directions down on a piece of paper, and needed to refer to it several times in the course of our two hours, for I have a woeful sense of direction and no memory at all for landmarks. Consulting this paper was difficult, because Dolores was always a restless girl who hated to stand still. When I stopped to check where we were, she would spin and fidget and attempt to go marching on while I was trying to unfold the paper with one hand and read "At rlwy bdg t rt onto bdleway".

But fidgets apart, she was fabulous. Not all horses are bold and confident on their own, but she seemed positively to delight in our solitude. At times we went lickety-spit along the straight bits; at others, I let the reins out to the buckle, so that they hung like the long stroke on the letter D, and we walked, at ease.

It was in those early rides that I learned her, or began to. I learned that she had a wonderful appetite to be up and doing: was always ready for a burn-up, would always give everything; and yet she could always take things more easily if I approached her right. She hated to be given orders, but was always open to persuasion. I learned that there were places that intoxicated her: where she had to gallop and where a halt was more or less impossible, for she was very quirky. The best way to deal with this was to avoid such places unless a mad gallop seemed a good idea. There were other places where we could take things in a more controlled way.

In short, we were coming to terms with life together. She liked a good deal of her own way, and I suspect now that this was why such a good little horse was allowed to go so cheap. I suspect, also, that there were other problems for an owner with ambitions to achieve big things in competition. These were to manifest themselves later in the most uncompromising form.

For this was a little horse with a very big nature. She had a rather overwhelming side. I always remember the time when some woman borrowed her without my permission, seeing what a jolly horse she was and how well behaved she was when you led her. The interloper wasn't ready for that extraordinary switch of personality: the way the Dolores turned from placid old thing to ball of fire the instant she felt your weight in the stirrup iron. She led her new rider a fine old dance, and she – the rider, not Dolores– came back terrified.

But I was never terrified, and it wasn't because I was brave. It was because, already, in those early days, I knew her. I had got the hang of her. It was not bravery: it was compatibility. She wanted to have a big say in what went on: so I gave her a big say. There were moments when I was very firm about my role in the decision-making process: that is to say, when we were on the roads with traffic whizzing six inches from her oversized ears. There were others times where I was prepared to take a consensus; and others, where she insisted on taking over, and I let her do so with a good will.

Now all this will reek of heresy to some horsepeople. But even then, I was riding horses to please myself, not to conform to any Platonic ideal of what a horse and a horseman should be. And besides, if you rode that mare in a different way, you would spoil her. Mare: note the importance of the word. Old horse expression: you tell a gelding, but you ask a mare. And I found that asking suited us both down to the ground.

Trust

I couldn't believe they were going to let me actually sit on the horse that was led out before me. A sleek, rangy chestnut, and as much like the horses I had ridden in Richmond Park as a Harley Davidson is like a moped. This was a thoroughbred, an ex-racehorse, and it looked lean and built for speed. I was out of my class. I couldn't wait. Fear and excitement were united, inseparable, in a fizzy, slightly sick-making cocktail. It was a taste I became increasingly familiar with.

I was in Hong Kong. I had recently moved there, in search of adventures, and this was one of the biggest, though not one I had anticipated. I had just wanted to keep on riding, keep the old Richmond Park thing going. But in Hong Kong, at that time, you either rode an ex-racehorse, or you didn't ride. I didn't know that. But I went out to try my luck at Dragon Hall, out in what were then the New Territories, and found myself confronted by the truth. You want to ride? Here's a racehorse. You want to fly? Here's a moon-rocket. Horseracing is big business in Hong Kong: and some of the retired horses get retrained by enthusiasts to do dressage and jumping. I was about to see the extent to which this retraining actually worked.

I was wearing jeans, ordinary shoes, a borrowed hat. I had an issue with riding clothes at the time, and besides, I couldn't afford the proper kit. And I remember the thrill of that first contact: the absolute certainty that I was, as horsey people say, over-horsed; that the horse was slightly too much for my level of skill and nerve. The idea was mainly thrilling: I hadn't known that horses like this were available to the likes of me. But I thought I could ride, I thought I knew what I was doing. I didn't know then that I had entered a different world.

Two important things happened on that ride. The first was that, with sweet, painful inevitability, I fell off. I was asked to canter gently up to the rise. I kicked where I should have squeezed; the horse took off with delighted and rather surprised enthusiasm and completely neglected to stop at the top. I was off balance when we hit the top of the slope, and as the ground fell away on the far side, so did I. I was heavily bruised, mildly concussed, and it took a week to get right.

But as we returned to the stables after my tumble, me back in the saddle, chastened but cheerful, I had another revelation. I was riding with a girl called Sally, one of the stable staff, cheerful, bossy, red-haired, rather pretty. And she opened my eyes as no one had done before or since: because this was the moment when my eyes needed opening. After the unfortunate fall and all that, we were walking back, and

Sally told me to let out the reins, to hold the buckle. To abandon all control. I had never done such a thing in my life. It was like letting go of the steering wheel of a car on the M25. Except it wasn't: the horse is a living thing, and capable of making good decisions. Sally said something to me, said it rather sharply, but with a brief, slightly electrifying smile, something she'd no doubt said a thousand times to a thousand other riders. And it has stayed with me. It is, perhaps, the founding principle of good horsemanship, and I have attempted to abide by it ever since. "If you don't trust your horse, how can you expect your horse to trust you?"

I took the words away with me and kept them. I also took my bruises and my ringing head. But the strongest memory of all was that incomprehensible explosion. Nothing accelerates like a thoroughbred horse: the nought-to-thirty in a stride is the biggest half-second surge of power that the average human can experience. And I had been part of that, I had experienced it, and my body and my mind were ringing with the memory of it. I had gone through another door; I wanted to do that again and again. I wanted that power.

Domination

Oh yes, they say. I know why you like horses. It's power, isn't it? Nudge-nudge, wink-wink, say no more. Whips, boots, spurs, bridles: that's what it's all about, isn't it? Nudge-nudge, wink-wink. I wouldn't totally object to a quid for every time I've had that conversation. It seems that an awful lot of people really do think that the whole point of the horsey life is using force to master a giant. Well, horses are giants all right, but I don't believe I've ever mastered a horse by means of force. I don't believe I've ever mastered a horse at all, come to think of it. Mastery never really seems to come into it.

Domination. It's an eerie concept. Many, if not most non-horsey people believe that the great charm of the horsey life is the opportunity to achieve complete domination over a giant. Your few stone over his half-ton: and you the winner, because of the aforementioned whips and spurs and so forth.

The only trouble with this idea is that it doesn't really work; and even if it did, it wouldn't be much fun. Oh, you can get horses to do what you want, in a rough and ready sort of way, by means of loud voices and heavy hands, and no doubt there was a good deal more of that sort of thing when horses were an economic necessity, rather than a luxury. No question, you can get short-term results by bullying, and horsepeople of a bullying nature can generally get somewhere. But I have explored the horsey world all over, out of curiosity, and while writing about horses for *The Times* and other publications, and time and again, when I find the top performers, I fail to find bullies. I fail to find people seeking domination. Quite the opposite, to tell the truth. I find people of a singular gentleness.

I heard a story about the great racing trainer, Aidan O'Brien, on his first day at the training establishment of Ballydoyle. He is a man tortured by shyness. His speech of greeting to his staff, it is said, went: "I'm sure we'll all get along really well and work very hard and make a great team, and if I find anyone raising a hand to any horse he's out."

Far, far, far more horses have been ruined by bullying than have been made by bullying. Bullying is only a pleasure to a bully: and most of the people I have met in the horsey world are not bullies. They are seeking something other than domination. The pleasure not in spurs and whips.

It can be annoying, dealing with the whips conversation. You can try agreeing. My joke about not having discovered boys yet generally works, if you call stopping the conversation working. A friend of mine called Kate used to say: "You should see the size of my horse's willy."

She said that one never failed.

But it's all nonsense. There is really only one reason for being with horses and that is, of course, power. But no, it's not my power over the horse; or even the horse's power over me. It's the power that the horse lends to you: that power that comes through co-operation across the boundary of species.

Delicate balance

She could jump all right. She was born to jump, bred to jump: a chunky back end, all the power behind the saddle. And what's more, she had strong personal views on the subject: she loved it. She didn't have to be cajoled, nudged, bullied, persuaded to jump: she had to be held back. She loved it that much. She was a mare for whom the normal restraints did not operate. She loved to fling her heart at a fence – and who gives a stuff what's on the other side? This glorious emotional commitment to the whole business of jumping was to lead almost to her downfall, but it was still a thing to be wondered at.

Like a football supporter or a National Hunt jockey or an intellectual or a Fleet Street sports editor, she had absolutely no respect for showjumping. She knew the poles would give way if you hit them. The best showjumping horses are almost pedantic in the care they take with their jumping: the finicky way in which they tuck up their feet, the way they sit back on their hocks in the approach, ready to uncoil. A showjumper is supposed to bascule over a fence, to roll over it rather like the coiled spring toy called a slinky.

But Dolores liked to charge, and if there was a row of fences in a straight line, it amused her to see how fast she could be galloping by the time we hit the last: and hit it we often did, with a terrible dispiriting clanking of poles. If I tried to fight for control, for my right to make a decision about speed, she would lose concentration and hit even more poles; and she knew this. She learned how far she could push: I learned how far I could pull. Thus it was that every round became a delicate balance between letting her do exactly what she wanted, or taking her on and fighting every step of the way. Not that she was defiant; it was just that the sight of a field full of jumps excited her beyond measure.

A better rider than me would have found some kind of solution: but then a better rider than me would not have bothered with this mad little mare. Me, I didn't give a stuff. I never actually won a single competition with her, though I picked up lots and lots of minor placings. And I honestly didn't give a bugger. If I had been more ambitious, I might have schooled harder; but a truly ambitious rider would have been best advised to sell her on and buy something less impulsive. I didn't want something less impulsive. I realised, right from the beginning, that I'd sooner lose with her than win with anyone else. I didn't feel that she was a vehicle I had chosen. It was nothing like owning a car. Instead, I felt that it was all something to do with fate: that this was the horse that was intended for me, and that there was nothing I could do about it. This was my task, my reward, my punishment. This was the horse to teach me, and the horse for me to teach. It was like an arranged marriage and there seemed to be no way out, even if I had wanted one.

Not that I ever thought about it. I just knew that this was my horse, and that there was no other. And so we would go to shows, every other weekend or so. I would arrive at the yard at some obscenely early hour, and Jan, the yard's owner, would be bossing us about as we got loaded into the lorry. I would groom, tack up, lead her on – she always marched on board like a little pro – and off we would go. Jan's lorry could take four horses; I normally rode with Jan in the lorry, while the others followed on in their cars.

We would arrive, park, get the horses out, tie them to the side of the lorry, leave them picking at haynets, while we put our names down for the events we wanted to enter. Me in my jods and leather boots, black jacket, white shirt, unremarkable tie. I would enter two or three events, pay my entrance fees. After that, it was time to mount up and warm up: for a horse is an athlete and needs to prepare mind and muscles for any strenuous task, just as a human athlete does.

And then, far too soon, and after far too long a wait, it was my turn and the tannoy announcement sang out – Simon Barnes riding Alive and Kicking – and I wanted to throw up the breakfast I hadn't eaten, and worried, more than anything else, about getting lost, forgetting the order in which I was to jump the fences, and so committing the direst of all crimes, letting the horse down. Sounds silly enough, I know, but this is, above all, a partnership, is it not? And, in any partnership, keeping your side of the bargain is what matters. All right, perhaps the idea of a horse's right to compete to the best of her ability is not really part of a deal you have talked over with the horse; but this false notion – that you might fail your horse – is a powerful and genuine feeling, and it makes for sharpened awareness and heightened concentration.

And then the edgy, cantered circle, and the bell that told us to go through the start and start jumping; and after that, a magic trick. It worked every single time. At the exact moment we came to the first fence, nothing existed in the universe but the mind and body of my horse and the course of jumps that lay before us. It was a physical thing, precisely like the throwing of a switch, and it came in the take-off stride, when I could feel her power bunch and collect as we prepared to take to the air for the first time: at which point my own body, in long-learned response, flung itself forward without reference to mind; my hands, also acting independently of voluntary control, yielded precisely to the thrust of her head, my eyes already fixed on the next jump. Tight turn, touch to steady her, and she was listening, concentrating, doing it right, and I knew the round would be perfect. Sound of her hooves in the receiving earth: pure and blessed silence from the non-falling poles; and then came the tiny patter of applause, the sound of one hand patting, and we were – she was, if you must – cantering through the finish. In a single stride, to show our perfect sympathy, we downshifted from canter to walk, and more pats, and now it was my task to keep her warm and relaxed and ready for the jump-off. High as kites, the pair of us.

Despicable me

We live in a nation of horse-lovers. It's the riders they can't stand. That's a conclusion I have been forced to come to after years of riding horses on the roads of Britain. Just about all the near-lethal experiences I have had with horses have been on the roads. If you ride a horse on the roads, you will meet, and on a regular basis, aggression, hatred, reck-lessness: people who are genuinely and repeatedly prepared to put horses and their riders in life-threatening situations rather than sacrifice fifteen seconds of their time.

Most people are fine; I must stress that. In the coun-tryside, a lot of people are brilliant. I wave and smile at every courtesy: thank you, thank you. I ride with considerable courtesy myself: sighting cars at extreme range and getting off the road to let them pass, never mind the wait; it's not only polite but safer for us all.

But every now and then, you get a driver who gen-uinely believes you have no right to be on the road, and then you are in danger. A horse is not a motorbike but a living creature. If you pass fast and close, the animal might well be alarmed and shift into your path. Also, a horse, unlike a motorbike, is capable of shifting three feet sideways in an instant of time. Therefore, it makes sense to pass wide and slow. The margins of errors are different with horses. Some people don't understand this; others are simply not prepared to compromise.

I have been in bad situations a thousand times. Only once actually hit: a driver rammed the horse I was riding – not Dolores, thank God, or we'd still be running – in the hocks. He took a bend flat out and was surprised to find me going around it in the same direction, but more slowly. Fortunately, the hysterical squealing of the brakes terrified the horse and he was in a flat gallop before the moment of impact, so, what with the car slowing and the horse accelerating, he hit us with not much more than a good bump. I was able to stop within 100 yards or so, the horse didn't slip and fall – always a strong possible on tarmac – and there was nothing in the way, so we got away with it.

On another occasion, I was taking a young horse onto the roads for the first time. I was in the company of an experienced horse, the right and only way to do it: the older horse as guide, protector and role model. Two cars got irritated by our slow progress, and hooted and roared their engines simultaneously. Nice move. The young horse was seriously frightened, turned around, rammed the horse that was supposed to be looking after him, and we all ended up over the wrong side of the road with cars in both directions forced to stop while we regrouped. The drivers swore at us for this confusion: bloody horses, shouldn't be on the bloody road.

I remember vividly a driver once coming at me at 60 mph. I waved my arm urgently to ask him to slow: this was seriously crazy. So the driver accelerated, and roared past giving me the finger. On another occasion –

But no. That's enough. It's just something you have to live with. Not only the danger of horses and cars on the same bit of road, but the hostility. Something very deep rises up in people: they hate you for being on a horse. Perhaps it goes back to some atavistic feeling that only nobs ride horses; that riding a horse is an expression of contempt for everyone else. If wishes were horses, beggars would ride, goes the old saying; it seems that the sight of someone on a horse brings to life some ancient rage: the peasant's revolt, Jack Cade, honest toilers pulling wicked barons off their horses.

But perhaps it's more basic even than that. Perhaps it's the fact that the horse rider is a long way up. You have to look up at horse riders, and they look down on you: so riders always look snooty, condescending, contemptuous. The fact that we are taught to ride with a straight back doesn't help. These days, no one sits with a straight back. From the ground, the classical riding position looks like the seated equivalent of the goose-step.

I remember when, owing to a miscalculation, I was unable to change into civvies on a trip into London. I found myself in a groovy pub in Islington called the King's Head. It was a time when everyone who was cool dressed in black with Doc Martens. I entered the pub in jods, riding boots and a horse-stinky Barbour. I was gazed at as if I had just evicted several peasant families from their tied cottages, murdered a dozen endangered animals, exerted my droit de seigneur on the village virgin, and would soon be reading *Mein Kampf* while nodding with solemn approval, wishing only that Margaret Thatcher were a bit less left-wing and soft-centred. This was not paranoia; it was the real thing: I was an object of mingled curiosity and loathing.

If you ride horses, you are going to be despised. You can drive a Porsche and be a man o' the people as much as you want; but ride a horse and you are a snooty, upper-class, arrogant, right-wing bastard who despises the rest of the world. I have always been uneasy about this, but not to the extent of wanting to give up horses.

Wealth

When I bought Dolores, I was living in a terraced house: a brief line of dwellings built on the roof of a railway tunnel. There was a small garden, but it wasn't big enough to keep a horse. The problems of stabling (kitchen? bathroom?) were also considerable. Access to the road could only have been through the sitting room. It wasn't on.

Not to worry. She stayed at Jan's. Jan not only bought and sold horses, she also ran a livery yard: that is to say, she provided a loose box and grazing paddocks, fed and mucked out and I gave her money. It was a damn good deal. There were plenty of other people who kept their horses with Jan, mostly divided into hunting types, who only turned up on hunting days, and a great raft of cockney girls who rather set the tone of the place. They came every day, mainly because they had to. They were DIYers, who did all the hands-on work themselves, buying their own feed, mucking out their own boxes, most of them competing at weekends. The lowest of the low: many a livery yard wouldn't touch them.

Most of them had jobs, of a non-fulfilling kind. The horses did the fulfilling, the horses were their vector for ambition. They drove unapologetic bangers. Such money as they had went on their horses. You don't need to be rich to own a horse: it's a matter of priorities. For them, the horses were first, cars and prestige and fancy gear and posh nights out came miles down the list. Some had boyfriends, others didn't, or they were never seen. It never occurred to anyone to ask: horses were always the absorbing topic of conversation.

It was a raucous place at weekends, or in the evening: loud with shouting and giggling and effing and blinding. I was accepted into the yard seamlessly. The girls helped me out again and again, when my somewhat sketchy practical skills failed me. Like all livery yards, it was a closed community with its own rules and customs: a doctoral-length thesis on the anthropology of the livery yard is long overdue.

The place was run-down where it was not actually falling down: crazy walls, cracked and peeling paint, just about everything on the yard fixed with baling twine. There were no hanging baskets, no mown grass, no white rails. You never knew what you would find there: sometimes a couple of coloured cobs herded in from a tinkers' marsh, sometimes an ex-racehorse fallen on hard times, at least once, a donkey. On one occasion the box next to mine was taken over by two small cows: Jan might have been doing a friend a favour, possibly in exchange for "a drink"; or she might have been trying out the cattle business. Jan was up for anything; so was her yard; so were we.

Her lorry was not one you'd be proud to park next to, but it got us to shows. I remember one time when Jan and I went to an indoor showjumping meeting. It was a filthy winter's day, the collecting ring (that is to say, warm-up arena) was outside, and when you went into the barn to compete, a man would grab your Barbour – filthy and stinking of horses as a good Barbour should – and you would go briefly into the dry to compete. We looked like the most fearful bunch of scruffs that had ever competed on horseback; we quite obviously hadn't got much in the way of small change, and yet we won just about everything that day. Me, Jan, two of the girls: we were unstoppable. I had a third and a second, so far as I remember.

And then we loaded the horses, all of us cold and wet and dripping, the rain quite unrelenting, and set off back to the yard, Jan and me in the lorry, the girls following in a banger. We unloaded, rugged up, put them away in their boxes, warm and cosy and tired and relaxed. Jan stayed on to feed them once they had settled. The only extravagance in Jan's life was horse-feed. We were great, us lot, we were fun, we were loud, we were cheerful, we were really pretty good – and by God, we were cheap.

Silly canters

When I only had an hour to ride, we would go to the wood and do the Silly Canters. Along the road, up a track (a gate on one side bearing the mysterious legend NO HORSE'S) and there was the wood. A path led before you, but it was not a straightforward one. It was turny, twisty, constantly asking a horse to double back on itself in its own length. There were a couple of more open places when you could kick on a bit, but mostly, the way was tight and complex. At one place, you crossed a road, and then there was more of the same, with a couple of fallen trees to jump if you were in the mood.

The path invited you to take it at a walk, perhaps while holding the buckle, to sit at your ease and muse on life's ironies. You couldn't really trot: you'd be going too fast to make a turn and have to stop dead. And so we didn't. We cantered.

We cantered every single step. Quite literally. It became a matter of pride: we would transition from walk to canter in the very stride in which we entered the wood, and then, in the most pernickety three-quarter time you ever saw, we would make each twist and turn of the path, expanding into a wild tumble down the hill and up the hill where it opened out, only to come back, at a touch, in a stride, into the plipperty-plopperty canter that we prided ourselves on so much. I sat deep into the saddle, making a million minute adjustments; she, weight right back on her hocks, cantering, at times almost on the spot, revelled in her mastery of balance, in her fantastic control.

As we hit the road, we would go from canter to walk, again in a single stride, cross the road demurely, looking both ways, and, the instant we passed from tarmac to earth again, we passed also from walk to canter: me steering with my legs, scarcely a touch on the reins. Back to the road, crossing it at walk, back into canter: finish the job. Dancing through the wood, dancing with the trees, dancing with each other: the ultimate form of country dancing, me sometimes laughing aloud at the wonderful absurdity of what we were doing.

It was not just fun in itself. It was also as a kind of virtuoso exhibition of our like-mindedness, of our understanding: of our sympathy. Was that a two-way thing? Who's to say? I only know that when we did the Silly Canters, the mare threw her heart into it, and revelled in her own brilliance. It was hard work for her, you see, all that balancing and concentrating and dancing, but she loved doing it. Were that not the case, she simply would not have done it: would have fallen out of canter into an easier trot, and then into walk. But she cantered, and I never had to do anything more than nudge with a leg to keep the canter going, even in the most forbidding circumstances.

She was a mare that was never concerned about easy options. She found her fulfilment in movement; movement was how she expressed herself. That is true for all horses, but that mare, she did a fair bit of her expressing while I was actually in the saddle. And that ridiculously silly way that we travelled through that wood: that went right to the heart of the matter. There was an absurdity in it that the horse herself might have been privy to. Certainly, that was the way it felt. I really do believe that I can say, in all honesty, that I have shared a laugh with a horse.

Call me a hack

Horses are part of the way we think, part of the way humans understand the world. You can tell this from the horsey terms still current in the English language. Words are things I am always aware of, being a hack. A hack, of course, is a journalist, a penny-a-liner: someone who knows he's not Milton or Shakespeare, but reckons he can put one word before the next as well as anybody else. OK, but no great shakes.

The word comes from a horse you hire: a hack, or to be more formal, a hackney. That is why a taxi is licensed as a hackney carriage. One suggestion is that suitable horses were raised on pasture near Hackney, in Middlesex. A hack or a hired horse will not win you the Derby, any more than you get a Ferrari as your hired car. By extension, to hack out, or to go hacking, is to ride about without any grandiose plans, and a hack is a horse eminently suitable for such a purpose. A racehorse trainer will observe the exercising of his string of racehorses from the back of his hack.

Before you set off on any major project, it is, of course,

essential to do the groundwork first. Groundwork is just that: the work you do with a horse while you are standing on the ground. You teach a horse to walk, trot and canter at your request long before you sit on his back. It is safer: it is also quicker, more direct, giving you more control of the options. And of course, horsepeople use the term to each other in its literal sense just as often as the rest of the world does so metaphorically: I've been doing the groundwork and he's going really well.

A riding horse that encounters problems may need you to do some work from the ground, rather than from the saddle. In which case, you will take him in hand. When you run an eye over a new employee, the first thing you do is to put him through his paces: see what he can do. In literal horsey terms, this means you get a horse to walk, trot and canter: the basic requirements. Anyone seeking to buy a horse for ridden work will first get on top and put the horse through his paces. From these paces you can see not only the horse's ability, but also his potential: how much more he can do.

Perhaps you have a friend or a colleague who is inclined to be impetuous, overkeen on his own opinions. You'd call him headstrong: a term borrowed from the horsey world, in which a headstrong horse leans on the beat, constantly asks to go up a gear, and is generally inclined to pull your arms out. With a headstrong human, as with a horse, the more opposition you give him, the more marked the characteristic you are trying to erase. In fact, keeping a headstrong horse on a tight rein is only going to lead to a fight, a confrontation. The secret of such confrontations is to give in while still winning. But we still talk about keeping a tight rein on the colleague, the budget, our ambitions, on anything.

Sometimes the best thing to do with a headstrong person or horse is to give him his head: to stop the fight and see how he copes with a little bit more freedom, a little bit more responsibility. With fighting, there is always the danger that you will put his back up. This is an uncomfortable phenomenon in the horsey life: a horse who has put his back up is bunched and tense underneath you, ready to throw in a buck without a second's notice. You can actually feel a horse's back arching underneath you, feel the state of extreme tension, and you know that something very unpleasant is likely to happen if you are not extremely careful. In such circumstances, I'm inclined to drop the reins – give him his head – and conspicuously relax myself, sit deep and easy, and aim to get the horse back into serious work without him really noticing. Make a point of any confrontation and you are generally going to come second. Best answer: don't put his back up in the first place.

A horse that is feeling the effect of a high-protein meal is full of beans: or he may be feeling his oats, particularly if he is a working stallion. Human two-year-olds don't leap about much: they toddle. It's horses of the same age that leap about like two-year-olds. But when they get older, the shape and angle of their teeth change, and they appear to become longer: hence long in the tooth.

If you pull up short on a horse, it's not just that you have made a sudden stop. The horse has stopped because he has gone lame. It is not the stopping distance that is short: it is the length of the horse's stride. It's a horrible feeling and you will generally get off and lead your horse home.

But say it's a good day. You get back to your yard in good shape. The horse has walked a long way since your canter, and is relaxed and cool. There is no sweat on the horse's neck. Everything is absolutely excellent: and you are home and dry.

Women in boots

If you like horses, you have to like women. It's compulsory. Absolutely non-negotiable. The horsey world is full of women, and if you don't get on with women, there's not much point in carrying on. My horsey life has brought me an immense catalogue, an endless Don Giovanni list of women I have known, women I have ridden with, women I have gossiped with, women who have taught me, women who have helped me, women who have given me good advice, women who have given me bad advice, women I have commiserated with, women I have congratulated, women I have listened to, women I have helped, women I have giggled with, women, above all, I have galloped with. It hasn't been an erotic or a romantic journey, with a single exception I shall come to in good time. Most of the women in my horsey life have been friends, colleagues, sharers of the horsey life. With many, I have had nothing in common at all, save horses: but if you happen to be taken that way, horses are an awful lot to have in common. The very nature of the horsey life seems to make for easy friendships across the sexes, and my life has been immeasurably enriched by the company of women in jods.

One of the myths of English life is that horsepeople are always tumbling in the hay with each other, that jods spend more time around your ankles than around your waist. Another equal and opposite myth is that horsey women are not interested in men at all: that they get satisfaction enough from a relationship with a horse. My own experience has been mainly of cheerful camaraderie and mutual assistance and tack room gossip and headlong charges across the countryside: and it's certainly been a life full of women.

But, of them all, perhaps I owe an extra-special debt to Gill. Gill was running Dragon Hall, the yard in Hong Kong where I first started to ride proper horses. I discovered almost at once that I would have to start from the beginning again. The intimidating nature of the horsey life put me off, but the lure of the horse made me go on. I didn't feel happy in the horsey world: I felt like an outsider: I didn't have the right gear or the right language or the right experience. I felt particularly uncomfortable working in the school: that is to say, in the sandpit going round and round in circles with women in jods looking at me. I wanted to get away; I wanted to be out in the country, where men are men and horses are horses.

Horsepeople have a not totally undeserved reputation for being sticklers for discipline, for insisting on doing things the right way and not the wrong way. But Gill understood, and her understanding made me a horseman. She took me outside, into the country, away from the school, and she taught me to ride as we went along: walk, trot, canter, gallop, jump. Gradually, I bought myself a pair of riding boots, a hard hat, eventually and at last succumbing to the wearing of jods. Then Gill persuaded me to work in the school. With her help and support, I started to compete.

And so I got more and more involved with horses, and I got more involved with riders. That is to say, women. The easy intimacies of the horsey life were comfortable almost from the start. There was always something to talk about, always an issue, always a crisis, always a joke, always a story: the horsey life is unendingly dramatic and, if you are the sort to be fascinated by horses, endlessly fascinating. The fact that it is all incomprehensible – both the language and the fascination – to outsiders subtly adds to the pleasure: the freemasonry of the horsey world binds us together. All the livery yards where I have kept my horses have been run by women: mad, jocular, devious, gorgeous, hilarious, brilliant, bossy, democratic, loud, quiet, sometimes superb riders, sometimes not. And they've all been great.

Of course, the womanliness of the horsey world means that a man who gets involved with horses will never get much respect from other men. Among my colleagues in sports journalism, I don't, alas, have a reputation for being a risk-loving, swaggering, booted tamer of horses. I'm seen as a bit of a girly. Girls ride horses and girls are soppy, right? So the horsey world is sentimental, risk-averse, and above all, tame. Of course, jockeys are respected, especially National Hunt jockeys, and cowboys are respected. But if you ride in this country, you are a girly.

But so bloody what? Horses are great and horsey women are great, and my life has been profoundly enriched by both. Many people believe there is something deeply wrong with horsey women. Au contraire.

Flying lessons

She never stopped. It was amazing. More than that: I see now that it was a miracle, nothing less. For she never looked to evade a jump. Every time you aimed her at a jump, she sought to fly. The thought of stopping or running out to one side never occurred to her. If there was a jump, you jumped. For joy, what else?

In Hong Kong I had ridden horses who would some-times jump, and sometimes not. Some wouldn't jump unless your approach was absolutely right: if the stride pattern was perfect, they would jump, if not, they would be unable to make the mental and physical adjustment. Some would jump if they liked the look of the thing, but not if they didn't. Yet others would jump if they were cajoled and nudged and encouraged, but not if you left them to themselves. Some hated the whole business but would jump, after a fashion, if bullied. Some, bullied, refused ever to go near a jump again. Some would jump, it seemed, to please the riders, others to please themselves. But with all the horses I ever rode over jumps, there was always a question at every fence:

will we make it? Or will we not?

I took on a horse that had been eight years a racehorse, and reschooled him – with considerable help – to do dressage, showjumping and eventing. We were a great success, but at every jump he needed instruction and encouragement, and every now and then, he would stop dead and explain to me that the thing was patently impossible. He could do it all right, but it was a fraught business for him.

Dolores did not deal in stops. She dealt only in flight. Not flight as in running away, as in the opposite of fight; I mean flight as in flying. If you got the striding wrong, she would try and sort things out herself: put in a short one, sometimes heart-stoppingly, see a bigger stride than you imagined possible and take off miles before the jump. She would always have a go, and if that sometimes made the poles fly in showjumping competitions, it was generally the rider's fault for messing up the approach. She bore this in good part and never dwelt on the error, never once thought about refusing a jump or two the next time round.

There are all kinds of ways of explaining such a thing. They tend to be couched in terms of an anthropomorphic morality: the horse is genuine, the horse is straight, the horse is generous, the horse is forgiving, the horse is, above all, honest. Such ideas may help a rider understand what is happening, but they don't add up in a horse's mind. The morality implied by terms like honest only means that the horse will do what the rider wants. What exists, in truth, is not a moral obligation but some elusive shared aim. What you always seek is a union of will between horse and rider.

Does the horse really jump to please the rider, or somehow to please himself? Impossible to say: all I know is that when I asked Dolores to jump, she jumped. Every bloody time. The process thrilled her, as it thrilled me: that I can say with complete certainty. But it took me a while to trust her as she deserved to be trusted. That was largely because I had grown used to riding horses I couldn't trust. It was also because I had been taught to ride with a modicum of control; taught to ride at a fence as if all the difficult decisions were down to me. It took me a while to realise that with this horse, there were no difficult decisions to make. If I wanted to jump the fence, then the fence would be jumped. All I needed to do was to ride with complete commitment, complete belief: complete trust.

That's what it comes down to. Horsemanship, I mean. In competition, in everything else. You don't get anywhere if you can't trust the horse: you don't get anywhere unless you can persuade the horse to trust you. Some people bring this about by violent and invasive means, others by means of intelligence and gentleness. But even the most oppressive of horsetrainers has to come to the point when he trusts a horse to carry him, to stop when requested, to jump.

That was the thing with Dolores. To begin with, when it came to cross-country events, when it came to the wildest discipline of them all, when it came to galloping about over the countryside, leaping whatever fence came our way, I was ever-so-slightly short on trust. I got more trusting with every outing: but what held us back was my own lack of trust.

Embracing Lilac

Lilac Chen changed my life. She was not a horsey woman. She was Taiwanese, best friend of my friend's wife. I was invited to the races by the friend, son of a racing high-up in Hong Kong, to join a party in a box, sit-down lunch and fine wines and all. In short, I was invited as Lilac's walker. This was not a hardship. Lilac was beautiful and delightful and funny: and we both drank quite a lot and talked an awful lot and giggled an awful lot more. We looked at the horses and made bets – like most Chinese, she loved a bet – and then watched the races and cheered and congratulated and commiserated. We won a few and lost a few more and we had a lovely time and even, occasionally, talked to other people in the box.

And then came the last race. We both decided to back the same horse, ten bucks to win. For the life of me, I can't remember why: perhaps it had a nice name, or a nice face, or perhaps Lilac picked it out and I went along with it because I was in the mood to go along with anything Lilac suggested. Anyway, it came in at fifty to one: we laughed, we embraced, we parted. It was a perfect afternoon.

I was left with a pocket bulging with cash: and I gave it all to Gill at Dragon Hall, and I told her I was now riding twice a week, and she was to tell me when I ran out of money. From now on, I was committed. I no longer saw myself as a person who sometimes rode horses. I was a horseman.

Being Clint

You get on a horse from the left, not the right. You get off the same side. You do so by taking both feet out of the stirrups and swinging your right leg over the horse's back. You only do this at the halt. You then remove the bridle and put on a headcollar, and do so in a manner that ensures that the horse is never free to run off. You then tie the horse up, using this kind of quick-release hitch. You attach the lead-rope not to the ring, but to a loop of baling twine attached to the ring: that way, if the horse gets frightened or stroppy and starts hopping about, it will be the baling twine rather than the lead-rope or the horse's neck that breaks.

You learn all this, and then you watch a Western and Clint gets off his horse on the right, and does so while keeping his right (ruggedly beautiful) boot in the stirrup until his left foot has touched the ground. He then ties the horse directly to a hitching rail, and does so with a single turn of the reins. And you wonder if the horse – or Clint – knows that everything is being done wrong. Or perhaps the question is: is doing it the wrong way actually wrong?

This obsession with a right way and a wrong way is an ineluctable aspect of the military traditions of horsemanship that still pervade the horsey life in this country. That's how armies, and therefore cavalries, work: everybody has to do everything the same way. If some people did it this way and some people did it that way, the army would be half as efficient. Armies do standardisation for the love of efficiency. They also do it for its own sake, of course: for simply the love of uniformity.

If you teach everyone to clean his rifle in the same way and at the same time, you ensure that all the rifles will be clean and available for the shooting of enemies. That's what armies are for. If you do the same thing with military horses, then the cavalry will be ready to charge when you need it to charge. No room for wacky freelancers, for loners, for temperamental artists. If one person got off on the right side while everybody else got off on the left side, you'd have people bumping into each other, getting in each other's way, unable to reach their weapons, and on, and on. Besides, the person who mounted a horse on the right would snag his sword on the saddle. Standardisation is essential for armies.

But, insidiously, the idea has spread. People believe that standardisation is also essential for horses. That you learn to ride horses by obeying certain instructions, by adhering to certain rules. Now there is a point to all this by-the-book stuff: and that is safety. Horses, as we have observed, can injure you, can kill you. And so the British Horse Society, for example, gives very firm guidelines as to how a horse should be managed: always load a horse onto a lorry with a bridle, never a head collar. That gives you more control. Quite right. Good instruction. But if you happen to know your horse, and you know the horse will load easily, then it's perfectly safe to load a horse in a head collar. Most people will load most horses in a head collar, unless the horse is unfamiliar or known to be dodgy: or they are trying to pass a BHS exam.

The BHS is right to insist that people who seek horsey qualifications learn the BHS way, because it is safer. It seeks to eliminate chance. But if you don't happen to be doing a BHS exam, and you don't happen to be a cavalryman, then horses will allow you far more leeway than you'd think. You can make your decisions. You can do it your way. Most of us have different aims than those of military commanders. My horse is not a cog in a military machine: my horse's job, if it can be so described, is to illuminate my life.

There is a changing culture, then, in horsemanship. The rule-laden stuff of traditional horsemanship is changing. That is partly because a lot of adults are coming into horses these days, sometimes taking on something completely new, sometimes picking up on something they had abandoned in their teens. And grown ups don't need to be told to do it this way, to do it that way. Grown ups are mostly in horses in order to enjoy a relationship with a horse. Unlike soldiers or children, grown ups can make their own decisions. And thus the nature of horsemanship is undergoing a quiet revolution. Not among the professionals, but among the quiet, four-million-strong army of people who ride horses for the fun of it.*

*Figures from the British Horse Society show that 4.3 million people ride at least once a year, and 1.8 million ride at least once a month.

Terror, please

We both knew what was going to happen. That was the trouble. Was it me, stirring her up? Was it her, excited beyond all measure? Was it me, caught between terror and joy? Or was it her, in exactly the same state? The start at a cross-country event was always a fraught time. I would tack up, get on board and warm up, doing the job thoroughly. I would seldom, if ever, take a practice jump – far too exciting – instead, I would perform dressage manoeuvres, changes of pace, tight, controlled circles, looking for flexibility and balance, control and purpose: getting her weight back, balanced on her hocks, because that's where the power in the jump comes from. And she always knew that there was something up: she would lean on the bit, head a trifle too heavy, my own corrections needing to be a little bit more insistent than at times of peace. She would seek to explode from walk to trot, and explode with redoubled force from trot to canter, so I would ease her forward and check with the same movement, trying to establish the best possible lines of communication. But all the time I worked, the worm of terror would be eating away at my gut: well, it is a frightening thing, cross-country riding. It's supposed to be. People can damage themselves quite easily in this sport. You head out into the country, just you and your horse, and take a series of obstacles, most of them specifically designed to terrify the rider.

Let's be quiet clear: this was not Badminton. This was the lowest level of competition: the local show. But the horses were still fast, the fences were still rigid, and the ground was still only fifteen or sixteen hands away and every bit as hard. Also – and this is a point to consider where terror is concerned – I was not as good as, for example, Mark Todd or Zara Phillips.

It would then be time to move towards the start box: two or three riders ahead of me, one about to start. It was here that terror turned into a rather unusually severe case of peritonitis. Time after time, I would say to myself: no, you really must stop. It would be foolish to carry on. It would be dangerous, and above all it wouldn't be fair to the horse. I would formulate ways of explaining things to the starter: I'm sorry, I have to withdraw, I'm unwell, the horse is lame, I felt something go. And the thing that terrified me still further was the absolutely certain knowledge that I was going to do no such thing. I was quite certainly going to go into that start box and start. Oh God. Oh bloody God.

It was here that things got borderline unmanageable. Dolores would be incapable of standing still at this point, needing urgent, unrestricted movement. She would throw her head around. She would dance like Fred Astaire. My control would get rather approximate: as we moved into the start box, other riders, other horses would move out of the way, giving us dark looks; occasionally the starter would have to leap nimbly to one side.

"Ten seconds."

Oh God, I can still feel the violent clutch of the hand in the gut, the vicious squeeze of the skeletal fingers. Trotting the mare in a mad little circle, to keep her busy, not pointing her in the right direction till the starter told us, because she might well get a glimpse of the start and set off unilaterally.

"Go!"

I loved above all the instant transformation of that moment. It affected us both, and did so profoundly. In one moment we were mad with terror and excitement, half out of control – in the next we were a sleek, well-organised, utterly unstoppable jumping machine. In a single stride we would be concentrating, all four of our eyes turned to that first jump: a reckless, out-of-control horse and a rider ditto would in an instant be transformed into a team of power and certainty.

At once, in an instant, the world was reduced to the course of jumps before us: a world a couple of miles long and one Dolores in width. I would be looking for the next jump even as we leapt the one before, and as we jumped, my hands would fly forward and I would leap with her movement to stay in balance, and on the far side we would charge away from the fence as if it had been nothing. She was filled with purpose, always: or rather, we were. That was the thing: the two of us with the one purpose. And our purpose was to fly: nothing less.

Not yours

It was shortly after Lilac Chen changed my life that Gill confirmed that the change had taken place. I was by then riding twice a week, thanks to the great betting coup, generally the same horse, an impetuous and sometimes scatty brown gelding called Ben Wyvis. He could jump all right: and gallop, too, as he once or twice did on the road, and several times elsewhere without being asked first. But a good lad: we got on well, and he and Gill taught me many things. I remember one moment when she asked me to jump up a staircase: giant steps carved into the side of a disused quarry, so that you jumped up and stayed up, and then did it again, but higher. The trick was to keep your weight forward. You needed to be seriously committed. If you were at all tentative, you would find yourself getting left behind; your weight too far back and slipping back further, perhaps disastrously.

I looked at the steps and thought to myself that this was insane; but I assumed that both Gill and Ben knew what they were doing, and kicked on, aiming for the middle. Commitment was the thing: commitment was the only safe option. Ben scuttled up as if pleased to be asked; I somehow stayed on board, and felt as if I had passed some kind of initiation test, that I was now Officially Mad.

We rode back. I changed and was drinking a cold beer – Hong Kong was always, at least for me, a fearfully boozy place – when someone asked Gill what she proposed to do next. "Have lunch," she said, "and then I will ride my horse."

Ride my horse. Ride *my* horse. Not ride somebody else's horse or anybody else's horse, but my horse. It seemed to me as outrageous a concept as leaping a horse up a flight of steps. And I was filled with an utterly dismaying pang of envy. I wanted to be able to say that, I wanted to say: "I will ride my horse."

But it was not precisely ownership that I craved. No: it was some kind of exclusive relationship, some kind of responsibility: above all, some kind of continuity. In Hong Kong, I had discovered horses, but now I wanted something more. I wanted to discover a horse. Mine.

Before I met her

Dolores was not the first. There had been other relationships with horses long before we came together. For getting
on for a year, I rode Ben Wyvis in Hong Kong. He was
exciting, impulsive, and had a good jump on him. There
was no formal arrangement: it was just that Gill, more often
than not, had Ben saddled up for me. She understood that
I was looking for continuity.

A few months after the Lilac Chen betting coup. I went
into formal ownership. In Hong Kong at that time, owning
a horse was not quite the same thing as actual ownership. It
was a kind of lease-hire arrangement. The horse was yours
to ride whenever you liked, within reason, but you had very
little say over any other aspect of the horse's life. I was the
greenest of novices, and it suited me pretty well.

And so I acquired a share in Favour: a well-behaved,
well-schooled, deeply obliging bay mare. The other share
was held by the Dragon Hall stables; Favour was useful to
them as a ride for those even less skilled and experienced
than I was. With Favour, I began to compete: she was a

careful jumper, who rarely stopped if you presented her at the fence in a sensible way. But rather better, I hacked her out alone. It was the first time I had ever been able to ride without someone looking at me: and it was one of those confirmation experiences. I was now absolutely sure that I was on the right track.

Favour and I were together for about a year. She was my schoolteacher and she was great. But I was full of ambition in those days and, after a time, I wanted a bit more of a challenge. So I took on a chunky dark bay with a white face: he was eleven years old and he had been on the racetrack for the past eight of them. He knew roughly two paces: walk and piss off.

His name, alas, was Fairy Fun: a worse name than Dolly, it has to be said. When we got to the competition stage, I was announced over the PA: "Next to jump, Simon Barnes and Fairy Fun." Well, I ask you. He was not in the least fairy-like: a decidedly earthy type, in my view. One day, when we were hacking out, I asked him to negotiate a precipitous downslope in trot. For any horse, this is a tricky thing to do: for an ex-racehorse, who likes to throw all his weight forward, in front of the saddle, it was asking a lot. But he found his balance and went down in a series of neat clever little steps, and so I sang to him as we descended: "Knock me down with a feather... Clever Trevor... either have they got, nor neither have not, got no right to make a clot out of Trevor."

So I called him Trevor, since he was clever, as a unique and personal stable name, and we had a great time together.

He stopped being a racehorse and started being a showjumper and we did a couple of two-day events as well, though the dressage was never that great. But he was great all right: and we had a grand time of it, and it was a sad thing to leave him behind when I went back home to England.

So I found myself living in a bedsit in Ealing, and I couldn't afford much to do with horses. However, circumstances improved eventually, and I acquired a half-share in a sparky old boy call Sunny, 14.2 and it was practically all muscle, and jumping muscle at that. (I acquired him from a Marlboro Girl, of all things.) A couple of times a week, Sunny and I would have a merry trundle around a bit of a park on the edge of London, and I would often put him at jumps that looked absurdly large for such a squat little horse. He flew everything.

His end was a rum business. Very suddenly, he acquired the habit of bucking. It was a complete change of character. You got on him, and he would buck until you got off or fell off. There was absolutely no choice in the matter: he would buck for ever. I tried to stay with him, convinced he would have to stop. He didn't.

Sunny's co-owner, Jean, ran the yard he lived in. She used him at weekends. For her gaggle of stable-kids, being allowed to ride Sunny was a real step up in the dominance hierarchy. But now he was unridable. We called the vet. I tacked Sunny up, took him to the sand school, sat on him, asked him to move forward and off we went. He bucked for a while until I came off. The vet looked at me and sneered:

"They're not very big bucks, are they?"

"The problem is that he won't stop."

"Here's what you do. Get a competent work rider"– the sphere of competence was clearly one that excluded me – "and put him on the horse. Get him to beat the horse until he stops bucking."

End of consultation.

Jean and I consulted each other after he'd gone. We agreed we'd do no such thing. We decided to retire him. Six months later he was dead.

Some time after that I was introduced to Dolores.

Being brave

Fear is part of your life as a horseman. Not all the time, not every day, perhaps not very often at all. But if you spend a lot of time around horses, you are going to spend some of it frightened. I remember, in my early days with Gill, thinking: "My God, I'm even frightened at trot." This was because the trot was big and booming and my control – that is to say, my balance and anticipation – was somewhat tenuous. Most fear comes when you are slightly out of control, and with horses, control is never total. There is always, with any horse at any time, the possibility of a serious loss of control. That, in a way, is the point.

Riding in cross-country competitions is only one way to find fear. I have also encountered fear, in heavy doses, working with young horses. A thousand times, I have found myself taking a series of deep breaths, trying to get respiration and pulse rate down, so I feel less frightened, so I give fewer messages of fright to the horse.

Perhaps the reason that the most peaceful moments you can have with horses – lazing through a lovely wood on a lovely day, holding the buckle of the reins, the world and your horse (my horse!) in the best possible tempers – feel so good is because they are set against the background of trouble and fright.

I knew fear as I learned to ride in Hong Kong; I knew fear again with Dolores in competition, and on many an occasion out hacking, when it seemed we had outcooled ourselves. I knew fear, lots of it, later, when the dreadful things began to happen – that was the worst. And I also came to know fear with two separate young horses: so much so that at times, I found myself muttering: "I'm sick of being bloody brave." Some say that courage is a wasting asset: so clearly, the truth is that I haven't been brave enough yet.

But fear is not the point. Certainly not the whole point. There are other adrenaline sports, extreme sports, in which fear is nine-tenths of the point. The purpose of such sports is not exactly the conquest of fear: rather, it is to make an accommodation with fear, to alchemise fear into a kind of ally, to reach that far-distant point at which fear becomes a positive force. After that, fear allows you – forces you – to find the right response. Through fear, you find the best of yourself. There was certainly something of that when I rode cross-country with Dolly Dolores: when fear led to the tenuous but perfect inner calm that took us around the course.

But with horses, fear is not the main point. Fear is more of an incidental. In one sense, it's the price you have to pay: if you want to live with horses, you must be a little bit frightened every now and then. But that's not completely right, either. Part of the *attraction* of horses is their frightening side. If fear is nine-tenths of the point of, say, whitewater rafting, then it is about one-tenth of the point of horsemanship. Of course, this figure climbs somewhat if you compete across country, go team chasing, ride in point-to-points, or go drag-hunting. But that's how it averages out: so that approximately one-tenth of the point of the horsey life is fear.

We are all just one ride away from losing our nerves. There's no ducking it, no shame in it. I have kept going because (a) I started late and (b) I've been lucky. Sometimes fear is deliberately sought, in competition, in mad gallops. Sometimes it strikes from a clear sky: generally when the horse itself gets seriously frightened. A wild horse is prey: it survives by running away. A horse is a flight animal and that means that the basic principle of his nature is fear, and when a horse gets frightened it has but one thought: run. Fear and running: a horse's two great intertwined and inextricable talents.

Most people in the horsey life have had hooves whizzing around their ears at one time or another: most of us have had that awful moment when we "hear" a kick: when we feel the swish of air go past our head from the turbulence of a flying hoof. There isn't a horseman living who hasn't taken a few kicks in the legs.

You learn how to keep these moments of danger to a minimum. You learn (and you should be rigorously taught, as the British Horse Society will tell you) how to play it as safe as possible. But it is not prudence alone that keeps you safe. Far more important, you learn to read horses. You learn, for example, that there are times when it's best to walk away. A thoroughbred playing up, stomping around his box, in the most terrible strop: "Show me what kind of horseman you are and change his rug," I was teased. "I'll show you what kind of horseman I am by doing nothing of the kind." Funk is usually more effective than confrontation.

I don't wish to exaggerate things, but there's no avoiding the issue either. The horsey life is never entirely free from fear: and that may just be the Tabasco in the Bloody Mary of the horsey life. But it's not the tomato juice; and it's not the bloody vodka either.

Madder by the day

The more I got to know her, the more crazy she became. I know why: I know precisely. What's more, I know exactly how I could have stopped the process. But I didn't know then. To be frank, I didn't really care. It was only later, when the whole thing got out of hand, that I saw where the road had always been leading. I comforted myself that there was nothing I could have done. But there was. I just didn't know enough, back in those days.

It was all a bit of a laugh, in the main. I learned new ways of riding, new ways of thinking, in order to accommodate her growing wildness. For example, she gave up any attempt at standing still when I got on. She was so keen to get going that the instant my weight left the ground, she would be off. I tried for a while to do the proper thing: refuse to mount, stop, get her to stop, put my foot back in the stirrup iron – and off she'd go again. Eventually I gave up. I learned to mount up while throwing my weight forward, anticipating her fast take-off, staying in balance, landing lightly in the saddle and then finding the iron on the far side.

Even coming home after a hard ride, she'd never quite relax, always walking a few steps and then breaking into a jog. So I let her reins out and gave her head at walk and, when she jogged, I gathered up the reins and brought her back to walk. Let out the reins, walk a bit, start jogging again, and I would repeat the whole process, time after time after time. Sounds a bit of a rigmarole, I know, but if I tried to check her all the time, she'd resist, and jog every single step, waving her silly head about.

She had the habit of anticipating the points where we cantered: so we'd make our approach in an unusual, perhaps a unique gait, the rocking horse-canter. She would canter more or less on the spot, showing supreme control and balance, while I would sit deep and check with the reins – gently enough; there was no need to fight her; I only needed to persuade her that now was not quite yet the time. Eventually, when we reached the point at which it was safe and sensible to go, I would aim her and she would set off as if launched from a catapult. The trick here was for the rider to anticipate the explosion and stay in balance, not to get left behind. (That had happened to me once in Hong Kong, when I had failed to stay in balance at a gallop that took us straight up an absurdly steep slope: I came off backwards, humiliatingly, and had to climb up to the ridge, using hands as well as feet, until I found the horse waiting with a rather sardonic Gill at the top.)

So I would generally take a quiet handful of mane, so that as she took off, she more or less hauled me into the best position, weight well forward, over her withers. I also began to thrust my head down and to the right of hers. I acquired this habit of riding asymmetrically, because when we galloped on the flat, or when I restricted her to a smart canter, she would sometimes chuck her head up. This manoeuvre has broken the nose of many a rider of many a horse, but I would ride slightly crooked, and time and again, her big, daft, overexcited head would thump into my shoulder. So far as I was concerned, this was all perfectly acceptable. It was the way she was. I could deal with it. It was part of her eccentricity, part of what made her who she was.

I knew one thing: there was no point in fighting. A few experiments on those lines caused her dismay and distress: she simply couldn't deal with being ordered about. She had to be understood, indulged, anticipated. That was her way; it always was her way; it was something deep in her nature. But it escalated; and it escalated needlessly; and it was a journey that led to disaster. But not all at once. Not immediately. And it was all such wonderful fun: until we got there.

Moral foundation

The two most important things to understand about horses are flight and herd. They are the guiding principles of a horse's life. Horses love to be together, and their response to almost every stressful situation is not to fight but to run.

The hardest thing a horse is ever asked to do is to move away from the herd. It is also the most basic thing humans require of a horse. A horse must submit to being caught and led out of a field, to being tacked up and ridden away from the stable. A horse must learn to work in a school while listening to a rider, not to the call of the herd; and if all goes well, he should also learn to hack out alone, relying on the rider for comfort and security and guidance.

Under the intoxication of togetherness, horses will do more than they can do alone. They will gallop round the Grand National course, and horses that have lost their riders will pick themselves up and gallop along with the rest. No horse ever wants to get left out. That is why the horses and riders who go round Badminton are the bravest and the best: because they will take on the most fearful of obstacles and do so alone, but for their riders. You can persuade a reluctant horse to jump by giving him a horse to follow. Hunting horses will perform miracles of bravery because they are many.

Horses are not solitary creatures. If you separate two horses who are used to being together, the one left behind will call piteously. You want the one you are working with, the one you are riding, to ignore the din, and to concentrate on you. The rider, then, must become, at least for a while, the herd. He must become the wisdom, the role model, the companion, the security, the repository of trust. He must become everything. It's the hardest thing in horsemanship: and the most basic.

In showjumping, the most difficult jumps are those that face away from the collecting ring, away from the temporary herd. The start box at a cross-country event asks the horse to turn his back on the herd and jump for his life: it is the single most stressful thing I have ever asked a horse to do. When hacking out alone, the trickiest task a horse must perform is to go past horses in a field, or go past other horses being ridden out.

One horse is no horse. A horse that is kept on its own will get miserable, depressed, off his feed, fail to get a kick out of life. If you have a lot of horses, then the composition of the herd is of vital importance. Most people will keep the mares in one field, the geldings in another, but that too can have its problems.

But flight is just as important. For a horse, running away is not shameful. Quite the reverse: flight is the honour and glory of a horse. Two horses, particularly if male-ish and youngish, will often compete as to who is better at running away: spooking competitively on the road at things that don't normally worry them at all. If they are allowed to go alongside each other, they will naturally have a bit of a race: a walking race, a trotting race, whatever kind of race they can: who is the best at running away? Me! Me!

Horses playing in a field will leap and buck, and perform all kinds of mad running-away games. Running away is not necessarily a response to terror: it is also a response to joy, to excitement, to the intoxication of being alive and with a fellow-horse. Every horse is an artist expresses his deepest being in movement: in flight. A horse has a pretty large brain and most of it is used to control movement. Movement, then, is not just a response to predators: it is also the heart and soul of a horse.

The miracle is that humans can share it, that horses will willingly allow humans to participate. The next great question, then, is why we should want to.

Lost

Jan's lorry always showed up late. We would generally arrive at a show with the first, and sometimes the second class already in full flight. There were disadvantages to this. The most important of these was that it was usually impossible to walk the course. Walking the course is your preparation. At the most basic level it involves learning the order the jumps come in. More advanced riders will plan how they are going to jump them.

In showjumping, you can miss out on walking the course and simply watch the other riders go round. It's not ideal, but you can get away with it. But a cross-country event takes place over the entire countryside, not just a small arena, and so there are areas, sometimes considerable areas, that are out of sight from the collecting ring. The organisers are good enough to number the jumps, so as you land – or even as you approach – fence 17, you can start looking out for 18. When you spot it, you go for it and hope for the best: and Dolores would always jump it, of course. But one of the problems is that you don't know what sort of jump it is. This is not the way to get the best from horse or rider, but at least we were out there and doing it. Obsessive ambition wasn't the way we managed things at Jan's.

So there we were at Potton, having turned up late. I had ridden there before, and knew the layout: but inevitably, they were always a few changes – the fences to be jumped in a different order, perhaps, or a new fence created, that sort of thing – to keep us on our toes. I managed to work out, from panicky collecting-ring scanning, roughly where the first dozen or so jumps were, and I trusted that the rest of the course would sort itself out.

And we were great, that day. We flew, we really flew. Nothing would stop us: nothing save my ignorance. I landed breathless in a small patch of grass and found, to my horror, that there was no fence in sight. That can't be right, can it? There must be a sodding fence. I had just cleared – just flown fence 17. Where the hell was 18? For a moment I dithered about, turning Dolores this way and that – and then suddenly there it was, right at our feet: a ridiculously small fence of half a dozen rough, slim pine trunks nailed together, hardly worthy of the name of jump. I turned her and squeezed with my legs, asking her to jump from a standstill, which is an unfair thing to ask of any horse.

But she did it all right. Of course she did. Now a four-footed jump – a cat jump, as it sometimes called – is a bastard to sit to. It has no rhythm, and of course, no forward momentum. These problems were made rather more acute when I discovered that it wasn't an easy fence at all. It was a drop fence: that is to say, the landing was a couple of feet lower than the take-off. I discovered this when I was still in the air, wondering why we hadn't met the earth just yet. And then we did. I found myself slamdunked crotch first onto the pommel, and in a blur of unspeakable agony, I lost my left stirrup.

I was furious. Not with Dolores – of course not, she had given everything, as always: but with myself, for my lack of preparation and non-existent sense of direction. I made three flailing attempts to get my foot back in the stirrup and then gave up in a wild temper: fuck it, who needs stirrups?

And so with one foot in and one foot out, I kicked on as I had never kicked on before: and in doing so, I discovered a new dimension of riding. She let herself go: did so without an atom of restraint. Fences passed almost unnoticed, we galloped, flat out, in a flash of bright bay limbs. I was riding with my nose almost between her ears: crazily overcommitted, one slip and I'd have been flying without the horse. But she didn't slip. We finished the course – the last fence a huge fallen tree – in wild extravagance. It took me two or three giant circles to come to a halt. At last, I was able to kick my right foot from the stirrup iron and jump down, mightily sore in the balls but with spirit soaring as never before.

What a horse. I had finally, through means of simple idiocy, found the best of her. I had found courage by means of sheer temper. I knew then that we could beat anybody. We were the best, she and I. Plans, glorious plans, burst and crackled in my mind. In the meantime, I paid the entry fee for the open class: the biggest of the day.

We were going to rip the bloody place in half.

Dolores and her dad

The urge to fly is an ineluctable aspect of the human condition. In one way or another, humans spend much of their leisure time and their dream time in search of flight. People spend a fortune on winter sports, which is basically a grown up way of running up to an icy puddle and going wheeeee. That freedom from the laws of friction feels like defiance of the laws of gravity.

I have written before, more than once, of my belief that all the non-confrontational sports are about the search for flight, or at the very least, the defiance of gravity: most team games have elements of the same thing, in the flight (note the word) of the ball. Swimming, the preferred holiday recreation, is of course floating, moving in three dimensions, a kind of flight.

Many drugs are lauded because they enable you to fly: "Gee, this acid is great, it's just like flying," as the neophyte said in the 1960s cartoon. Birds are the most studied organisms on earth. We talk about the soaring nature of human aspiration, about flights of fancy. The most holy places on earth are invariable lofty, soaring structures that reach sky-wards in multi-pillared glory. We seek a vividness of experience that goes beyond the limitation of the human frame, of the human condition. We seek to escape: from the earth, from our limitations, from our own natures, from our base selves.

And, if you have ever galloped a horse, you know the best way of doing it. If you've ever jumped a horse, you know the same thing. If you've ever ridden a really good dressage horse, and felt the utterly improbable elevation in trot and canter, you know what I mean.

To do anything at all on any horse is a form of flight. First, your head is much higher than normal. What's more, you can go faster and travel further than any footslogging human, and do so in a gloriously non-human kind of way. In C.S. Lewis's book, *The Magician's Nephew*, one of the Chronicles of Narnia, Strawberry, the cab-horse, becomes Fledge, the father of all flying horses, and Polly and Digory ride on his back to a great adventure.

There are many more things that horses can give beyond all this, but the horse's gift of flight is part of the extraordinary package that comes from horse to human. With a horse beneath us, we can indeed fly. We can go faster than any human, yet without an engine, without a device of any kind, just with the willing complicity of another living soul. Knees into the saddle roll, bum in the air, hands low, teeth in the mane, every muscle of your body moving in rhythm to that of the horse, so that it's hard to tell where you begin and she ends, at least for as long as the gallop lasts: then you slow and stop (at least that's Plan A; Dolores would often direct you towards Plan B, and even C and D), patting a sweaty neck, mouthing nonsensical endearments, fizzing with glorious repletion, letting the reins out till you clasp the buckle, because you know that trust is a two-way street. Nothing better in the world: except the next time. Oh yes, every horse I have ever ridden is Pegasus, though I suspect that Dolores was his best-loved daughter.

An incompetent rider

O'Malley also loved Dolores. He was a big horse with a big white face: Irish draught cross thoroughbred, alarmingly heavy, not to say lumpish in front, surprisingly athletic behind. Dolores always enjoyed male company, and she and O'Malley were an item. Not that O'Malley could do much about it, in practical form, but they were inseparable. This was handy for me. Jan's big fields were always full of horses, many of which were temporary residents, for Jan bought and sold horses more or less on a daily basis. It is hard to pick out a single bay horse from a vast herd, but O'Malley was recognisable across a dozen acres. So when I went to ride, I would take up my head collar, look for O'Malley's white face, walk across the field, and there, every time, was Dolores by his side. They were a touchingly faithful couple.

O'Malley was owned by Theresa, one of Jan's cockney clients, and like most of them, she earned very little money, drove a banger, and had a fabulous horse. She and I sometimes teamed up to ride in pairs events: the horses always enjoyed competing alongside each other; and O'Malley, sometimes a reluctant jumper and inclined to be sticky in between fences, would come out of his shell and give of his best when Dolores was around.

It was because of O'Malley's sometimes indifferent jumping that I had a profound lesson in many difficult subjects. Dolores and I were doing pretty well, it must be said. Theresa thought this was because I was a rather fantastic rider, a point of view I was inclined to go along with. So she asked me if I would do her a favour and ride O'Malley in a cross-country competition. I said I would be delighted, and one evening, the day before the event, I jumped on him to ride him in the school while she watched me work my magic.

It was awful. I was awful. I couldn't do a thing. He was a big, uncoordinated bugger, nice nature, but he needed bossing about. He needed to be held together with firm hands and very strong legs. He needed shoving forward into the bit with great emphasis. He needed the will of an assertive rider. All in all, he was the exact opposite of Dolores. I had neither the technique nor the temperament to cope with him. I jumped off him after ten minutes. "Theresa, I'm sorry, this is hopeless. I can't do a thing with him."

"I noticed."

There are several points of interest here. The first is the truly shocking fact that every horse is different from every other horse, and must be treated as such. I have had many chance rides in my life, but every time, this essential truth of the horsey life has taken me by surprise. There is always something about the way a horse moves, responds to its rider, to the environment, to circumstances: its stride length, the nature of its transitions, the elevation of the gait, all manner of small things that add up to an individual unlike any other. Broadly similar to some, perhaps, but essentially unique.

And naturally, there are some individuals you get on with better than others. My nature suited Dolores, who could never bear to be bossed about. Any restriction brought out the worst in her. Now the better a horseman you are, the better you can adapt to different horses and the faster you can understand them. The more you can anticipate their responses and pre-empt mistakes, the more effective you will be, in any discipline, from a quiet hack to Badminton or the Grand National.

I was out of my depth with O'Malley, and that taught me about my own limitations, and about the limitless variety of horses. But also, it made me understand how truly blessed I was with Dolores: to realise that I had found, almost by chance, a horse that suited my nature so profoundly, so perfectly.

Taking wing

We met, we talked, we kissed, we fell in love, we made love, we broke up traumatically, we were reconciled still more traumatically in the midst of a thunderstorm, I proposed marriage, I was accepted. But the second week was a good deal quieter, so we went riding.

We had met before. I knew Cindy as a friend's sister, a not ungorgeous girl with eyes to die for. She possessed a wonderful gift: that of listening to me while I talked about horses. I kept her fascinated, or at least quiet; it was my first experience of her almost infinite generosity. She used to ride herself, and kept horses at home, when she was younger: which made her ideal for talking at. Then things changed one dramatic night, as things sometimes do.

After we got together, she took up riding again. I was still living in Hong Kong at the time, and she was a neighbour (not that she saw her own place much after a bit) out on Lamma Island, which lies just to the south of Hong Kong Island. A couple of times every week, she and I would make the long journey out to the New Territories: three hours there and three back, the ferry from Lamma Island to Hong Kong, the tunnel bus, the train to Sheung Shui, which in those days still ran on a single track, and then the taxi to Dragon Hall, where my own ex-racehorse stood waiting in his box.

They let me hire another for Cind, and trusted us to ride out without escort. And so, together, we rode out around the glorious countryside at Bee's River, hard by what was then the Chinese border, a place of precipitous hills and mad vegetation. And we walked and we talked and we galloped and we pulled up glowing with the glory of it, and eventually we got back to Dragon Hall and then went to eat lunch at an extraordinary restaurant called The Better 'Ole next to Fanling station, and then got the train and the bus and the ferry back to our island.

Oh, courting on horseback, it's the only way, of that I'm convinced. The physical intensity of horseriding and the languor that follows seems to me an essential aspect of being in love: also, the long opportunities for conversation while you are both looking straight ahead and both with at least half of the mind and most of the body in tune with an animal: these things make for a unique intimacy. We learned all and everything about each other on those rides, though sometimes we just giggled. And then at the bottom of the steepest slope we would kick on and gallop, last one on the top's a cissy, and pull up laughing and patting and sweating and filled with shared delight. There's nothing like it, for sure.

Sometimes the state of being in love is depicted as a

kind of flight: as if gravity had been defied, or better still outgrown, like the floating lovers of Chagall. Some years later, I read *So Long, and Thanks for All the Fish*, the fourth part of the Hitch-Hiker trilogy, about Arthur Dent and Fenchurch: and how they stepped from the high window of Fenchurch's flat and made love while floating across London: "In a mute embrace, they drifted up till they were swimming amongst the misty wraiths of moisture that you can see feathering around the wings of an aeroplane... Arthur and Fenchurch could feel them, wispy cold and thin, feathering round their bodies, very cold, very thin. They felt, even Fenchurch, now protected from the elements by only a couple of fragments from Marks and Spencer, that if they were not going to let the force of gravity bother them, then mere cold or paucity of atmosphere could go and whistle."

Well, that's how we felt, when we rode out in the embracing warmth and sweat of the advancing Hong Kong summer, the two of us floating weightless above the surface of the earth, supported only by love and hope and horses: but knowing these things would sustain us for years and years.

Too near the sun

So we flew. We really did fly, that day, she and I. That day at Potton was the best. I knew that before the start. It was the Open class, and some of the fences looked pretty big, and of course, I had not been able to walk the course, and there was no time to do so between classes. But, after my first and semi-disastrous round, I knew the layout: it was mostly a matter of remembering to jump the big fences rather than the small ones that generally stood alongside. There were a few extra fences, but I could see most of them from the collecting ring. It was going to be all right.

Dolores was up for it all right. Her initial craziness had been run off by our earlier round, but she was fit and hard and ready to rock. For her, the usual fidgets at the start; for me, the usual terrors: but both muted, at least to an extent. The terror was important and so no doubt were the fidgets, but I felt full of purpose. Full of certainty. We both did. I know that. It is simply not in the arena of debate: I knew the horse, and I knew me.

I kept her on a shortish rein in the start box, but I

didn't fight her as she made some silly little circles and sideways curvets and little hops, or when she took her front feet off the ground for a second to two, or when she went into rocking-horse canter. I knew she would be full of direction and purpose the instant I looked at a fence and thought about jumping. They say that riding some horses over fences is just a matter of point and kick. With Dolores that day, it was pared down still further: just look and think.

Perhaps power of thought alone is enough to transmit your intentions to a horse so perfectly in tune with its rider: more likely, the act of thinking about jumping creates a subtle, unconscious all-but-indiscernible (except to the horse) shift in muscle tension and in the position of upper body and legs and hands. I don't know, to tell the truth; all I can say for certain is that I knew, back in the start box, that the instant the man said go, I would look at the jump with meaning, and in that instant we would cease to muck about and would be moving towards it as an unstoppable force.

Go.

And we were off on the round of a lifetime. I remember almost nothing: nothing of the detail, anyway. I do recall one massive jump made of straw bales, and I remember thinking, that's remarkably big. I noticed it as you notice a tree that is bigger than the rest: as a mildly intriguing observation. I certainly didn't notice it as anything difficult or challenging. I was thinking as Dolores thought, seeing the course as she saw it, and I knew it was nothing, or nothing much. I didn't slow her or steady her or do anything intrusive at all: by this stage, we were beyond all that. I just looked at the jump and she did the rest: standing back a massive distance so I thought for a second that we must land on top of it or even in it, but somehow we were still rising as we met the jump, and I thought, quite coolly, that it was an awfully long way down, and then we were on the far side and I was already looking for and then looking at the next fence.

What I remember of that round is its totality. I remember the flow and rhythm: the inexorable logic of the way fence led to fence, the way leap led to leap, the way clearance led to clearance. I remember also the way my balance and hers seemed but one thing: at each landing, I was with her; at each take-off the same, at each stride, I was moving with her. My mind had become hers and hers mine; two instruments, one tune; not harmony but unison.

And we cleared the last, the same fallen tree, but we had to leap it at a point where it was higher and wider, and we cleared it as if it were a twig. We pulled up in triumph, and I dismounted and unsaddled and walked her in a sweat rug till she was cool and dry, saw that she had hay and water, and then I went to collect our winnings. We were third, of a class of 50. I was a given a cheque for five pounds and the glory of it has lasted for ever.

And what might we do next?

I'm serene, you bastards

I had an awful day the other week. I was researching a piece for *The Times* to a tight deadline, and every two minutes the internet connection dropped. I didn't deal with this at all well. I shouted, screamed, swore. I was impossible to live with. I finally got the job done, and spent the rest of the day with a tension headache that felt like a tourniquet on my skull. I'm a bit like that. Things get on top of me. My life has contained a million instances of impotent rage at mechanical objects. I am quick, volatile and have a nought-to-sixty temper, one that's generally gone as soon as it starts, but leaves me wrecked. Others, too. There are no small disasters in my life.

Right at the start, when I started riding thoroughbreds in Hong Kong, I made the most extraordinary discovery. When I was around horses, I didn't scream and shout when things went wrong. On one of my earliest rides with Gill, a horse I was riding – it was the laddish Ben Wyvis – got upset with the traffic. He did an instantaneous spin through 180 degrees and galloped back along the main road to the stable in a crazed panic. I stayed with him; I had him steady within 50 yards and stopped not much further. I then turned him back into the traffic and walked back to where Gill was waiting with a big grin of both relief and, impossibly, admiration. I didn't understand why. I didn't think this was a big deal at all. It seemed to me a very straightforward and simple thing to do. I was completely without stress. And when I thought about things, I realised something wonderful: that my lack of stress had miraculously communicated itself to the horse. I had told him, just by sitting quietly, that the traffic that had upset him so much was in fact no big deal.

When I came to ride Dolores, this sort of thing no longer came as a surprise. I found the same bizarre calm in the midst of her excitement and nonsense. Now please be assured here that I am not boasting. It is not a matter of courage or excellent riding skills. Rather, it is a quirk of temperament. When I am with horses, I find an unexpected and underused side of my nature. Cind will give a hollow laugh if you talk about my serenity: but Dolores will know exactly what you're talking about. It's just the way I am with horses. Perhaps that is at least one of the explanations for the addictive quality of the horsey life: that I need the calm, that I relish the calm and that I can't find it by normal means. That makes it the opposite of being an adrenaline junkie: though at least a part of me is that as well. But the strange combination of adrenaline-fuelled excitement and rather melodramatic serenity are each a part of the horsey life, so far as I am concerned.

There is a story in one of the millions of books about

understanding horses in which two similar incidents are compared. Both concern horses being led in a head collar; in both stories the horses are seriously spooked, and both of them act up. Owner One loses her temper, shouts at the horse and hits it, with the result that the horse gets more and more upset and has to be put back in his box to calm down. Owner Two does nothing: stands there while the horse runs round and round in the tiny circles allowed by the lead rope. The horse slows, stops, is patted, made much of. And life continues.

Now, for once, I can be the good guy in the story. I have found myself, time and again, still and calm and doing calm things in situations that look crazy and ultra-stressful. And, for an unquiet man, that is really rather a marvellous thing. Often, when Dolores was in one of her over-the-top moods, I would just throw the reins at her: telling her, do whatever you like, it's all fine with me. And she'd relax, as much as she ever could. She'd never ever give up if you gave her a fight.

Horses respond to each other. Communication is what horses do: it's the herd thing again. The exchange of information and the infectiousness of mood is the way horses live and think and act. I have seen it on Newmarket Heath: one horse spooks, so they all spook; and there may be 50 of them altogether, starting at nothing. You can see the good stable lads doing what I would do: absolutely nothing. And you watch horses in a field: one horse wants a mad five minutes so they all join in, charging about, performing handbrake turns, bucking and farting and putting their hind legs higher than their heads. Sometimes a horse will roll: so they are all suddenly in the mood for a roll. A human works with a horse by means of the same channels of communication. That means that if I am calm, the horse is likely to be calm.

Dolly's excitement was her gift to me, my calm my gift to her. Or was my calm a gift that came from her to me? And was her excitement anything to do with me? Impossible to know. All I can say for sure is that when she went crazy, I dropped the reins and laughed. Not my courage, not my skill. Just my nature. And hers.

Suffering sadness

Love is not only about the good bits. In fact, the idea that love is only and always fun is one of the great heresies of 21st-century life. True, love frequently begins in fun – James Joyce talks about "the game of laugh and lie down". But if you discover nothing more than fun, then it wasn't love at all. Just fun. That is true of love between one human and another: it is also true of the love of a human for a non-human creature. There is a moment in *A Dance to the Music of Time*, Anthony Powell's twelve-novel *roman-fleuve*, when the narrator, Nick Jenkins, meets a lovely girl: "Would it be too explicit, too exaggerated, to say that when I set eyes on Isobel Tolland, I knew at once that I should marry her? Something like that is the truth; certainly nearer the truth than merely to record those vague, inchoate sentiments of interest of which I was so immediately conscious. It was as if I had known her for many years already; enjoyed happiness with her and suffered sadness."

Many little girls will go through "the horsey phase". For some, it is merely part of growing up, and I think a good one. If nothing else, it is a way of learning about the complexities of relationships which are often gratifying, sometimes difficult, sometimes troubling. And sometimes, for that matter, fun. The horsey phase is an apprenticeship, and the greatest lesson you can learn is that you can't, ever, have love on your own terms.

I remember attending a Pony Club camp. I was there as an observer, researching a piece for *The Times*, but it is impossible merely to observe a Pony Club camp. You find you have ponies to catch, little girls to help back onto ponies, little girls to whom you must recommend deep breaths as a specific against tears. Love without tears is like alcohol-free lager.

By the time of our triumph at Potton, I had already experienced the non-fun side of life with horses on many occasions. Sometimes your horse is lame, and you can't ride. Sometimes this happens before a competition you have long been looking forward to. Sometimes you get kicked. Sometimes your foot gets trodden on: bloody hilarious, that is. Sometimes you are simply not good enough to get your horse to perform as you would wish. Sometimes your horse, after doing it perfectly last week, no longer wishes to co-operate. Sometimes, before a jump, your horse stops dead or ducks sideways. It's awful. It feels like a betrayal. Sometimes it is; but, mostly, you have to face the fact that it is you that has failed: bad riding, failure to see a stride, failure to get a horse balanced, failure to be in balance yourself, failure to move together with power and purpose.

And sometimes you fall, and you collect your bruises or

worse, and mostly it is your fault, but sometimes it isn't, or it doesn't seem that way. And you either give up or you carry on. Life with horses is not all gallops and patting and jumping and long walks through the woods, any more than love is all tumbling in the hay and galloping knee-to-knee with your beloved.

All the same, I wasn't prepared for this.

A little over the top

After Potton, business with *The Times* took me away from home for just under three weeks. In late spring when I got back, the last meeting of the cross-country season lay ahead, and it was at home, at Jan's place. We knew the course intimately. We would gallop as we galloped at Potton: no one else would have a chance. Everybody else was competing for second place.

I knew she would still be fit when I got home, because a friend from Jan's yard had agreed to ride her while I was away. This was good. So I got back to the yard on a Friday with the competition the following day, and we hacked out through the woods.

Lord, she was crazy that day. Crazier than I had ever known her. Rocking-horse canter in the road. Flinging her head into my chest. Dancing like Fred and Ginge. And when we went into the wood to do the Silly Canters she was all over the place, leaping and plunging and bucking. It took a fair bit of riding to stay with her; well, I was impressed, anyway. It didn't feel dangerous exactly. It was, on the whole, rather funny, in a crazy sort of way. But it took my breath away a bit. At one moment, the ride takes you along a road from one bit of wood to the next: and here she briefly stood on her hind legs, to the dismay of a friend who was riding in the opposite direction. "Are you all right?"

"We're great. Just a little over the top."

"Are you sure?"

"Nah, she's great. No worries."

And then another mad session through the wood. She came back drenched with sweat, and I was not entirely dry myself. I got off just a little bit in awe of her. That really was a quite stupendously silly performance. But no matter. She'd be a different horse on Saturday.

She was.

Betrayal

Betrayal lives in every relationship based on trust; and beyond question, a relationship between a horse and a human depends on trust. Can a horse, then, betray a human? Rather a large question. Let us start with certainties: unquestionably, a human can betray a horse. I know, I've done it. So has everyone else involved in horses: just as everyone who has been involved in a relationship based on love has betrayed and been betrayed.

There is a deal involved in all relationships: an unwritten contract, one in which new terms can be negotiated, but which insists that certain laws cannot be transgressed – at least, not without cost to both parties. The rules vary according to the people involved, and they change, too, as the relationship itself changes. And certainly, in any cross-species relationship involving a human, the human can fail the other party: for it is always in us to betray. It is, if you like, an aspect of rationality.

There are many little betrayals in every relationship, but I remember a gross betrayal of Trevor. We had taken part in a showjumping competition the previous day, and I had taken a spill at a particularly intimidating double – two white gates, each with a giant red spot in the middle. Trev had never seen anything like it before. I sensed his hesitation, urged him into the jump; he overcame his nerve, advanced boldly, but at the last second, he bottled it. Stopped dead, made a half-turn right at the same instant, and I took the fence alone, arse first, sent it crashing to the ground as I hit the top rail and collected bruises of thrilling shades of yellow and purple. You could call that a betrayal, I suppose: but you could also, and perhaps more accurately, call it a misjudgment on both sides.

The real betrayal came the following day. The course was still up, so I and a few others who had had problems went to put things aright. Our instructor, not Gill, but a new girl, a different Sally, told us to beat our horses until they jumped. I went along with this. In the end, he jumped. It took a lot of beating: my arm was tired. I don't know how Trev's arse felt, but I can guess. I don't think either of us really deserved our soreness.

I had never behaved like this with a horse before, nor since. I should have said, No, Sally, I'm not doing this, I'd sooner not jump if I can't persuade him to do so by any other means. But I didn't. I administered the beating. This was wrong: the trick in teaching a horse to jump is not to over-face him, frighten him, then punish him for being afraid. The trick is to give him confidence. Even if you care nothing for equine welfare, it was bad training. It wasn't going to lead to better results: and in fact, it didn't.

It is not so much that hitting a horse is in itself wrong, though I am not a great fan of beatings. Rather, it betrayed the relationship we had. The balance was altered. I had treated the horse as a friend: now, out of the blue, I was treating him like a slave. As a result, he didn't know where he stood. I had confused him thoroughly. I was a bit perplexed myself: after all, why did I have a horse in the first place? To jump when I tell him? To act as my vector for competition and victory? Or to have a cheerful and fulfilling relationship?

Put like that, the answer is easy. For me, anyway. But I didn't see things with anything like that clarity then. I didn't know much about the horsey life, I didn't know horses all that well, I wasn't used to making my own decisions with horses. I thought that this was what you were supposed to do: that if you didn't behave in an occasionally violent fashion, you couldn't live the horsey life. And I wanted to live the horsey life. So I went along with what I was told; and it was a small but significant act of betrayal.

I am not at all sure whether or not a horse can betray a human. Certainly, it can seem like it. A young horse kicked me, hard, when I was rugging her up, and I thought she knew better than that. I was inclined to see it as a poor show on her part, but all the same, I had to admit that I had just overloaded her with stressful things. It was raining, it was late, it was pitch-dark, it was windy; and putting on the rug was one too many things to deal with. She could have done better, but then so could I. Not a betrayal: another misjudgement, a failure to get inside the horsey mind quite as I might have done.

On another occasion, the kindest mare I have ever known bit me between the shoulder blades, stabbing out from over the stable door, just as I turned my back on her. It was as if Postman Pat had gone for me with a flick knife. I was wearing five or six layers of clothing for the hard weather, but she still managed to draw blood. I was aghast, felt betrayed. But there was a reason: she was carrying a painful injury and had been shut in her box for many days, and she just lost it. She seemed as confused as I was. It was as if she had been, for a single moment, possessed by a devil, which instantly vanished and left her herself again. It was an aberration: bewildering, but ultimately understandable. Forgiveness, or if you prefer, the re-establishment of mutual trust, was an easy thing; but it was a week or so before I turned my back on her again.

There are ways in which a horse can disappoint you, and we invent terms to cover the situation: we talk of a dirty stop, we say that the horse is not genuine, is not honest. I can empathise with them all, because there are times when a horse does seem to let you down: when justified expectations are simply not fulfilled; when it seems that the horse does not complete his side of the bargain. Sometimes this can be dangerous. Sometimes – often – it is the result of bad treatment, insensitive training. But sometimes – rarely, rarely, but sometimes – for no apparent reason, a horse cannot or will not meet his half of the deal. In such circumstances, any attempt to bring him round is foolish to the point of being life-threatening. A horse that invariably bucks his rider off or bolts at the least provocation is not safe. And who will pay the money to keep such an animal alive and fed and housed?

My black and yellow shirt

When I competed across country, I always wore an ancient hockey shirt; black with yellow sleeves. I still have it. I borrowed it from Simon Akers-Jones 30 years back and, alas, he won't be asking for it back. He lent it to me when I rode my first cross-country event. He was a neighbour of mine in Hong Kong. He was in his early twenties, a person of great thirst and great sweetness of nature. He had a taste for excess in many ways, but he never lost his innocence, his elephantine gentleness. He had a job that he hated; he said that he had only ever been happy when working with the dolphins in a local theme park. We shared many a beery night, but there was always a certain quality of sadness behind his jollity. When we were no longer neighbours and I seldom saw him, he met a lovely girl and seemed to be coming to terms at last with grown-up life. That was when he died: wiped himself out in a single-car accident. I hung onto the shirt and have always thought of him when I have worn it.

I was wearing it when I arrived at Jan's for the cross-country competition: striding up in my jods and my boots, flat cap on my head, hard hat in my hand. I was bursting with confidence: and the confidence of a rider always inspires the horse. I was to enter the small competition and the team event on the Saturday and have a dart for the big competition the following day.

I went to greet Dolores in her box. She was, as always, calmness and gentleness itself. It was only once she had a rider on her back that she changed into something else; to mount her was like taking Clark Kent into the phone box, a moment of magic that I always loved in her.

I led her out and got on board. The expected transfiguration took place, but I knew how to deal with that; we both did. I walked her down, through the crowds of spectators and competitors, horses and horse boxes, the place alive with banter and nerves and last-minute instructions and the click of hooves and the boom of the tannoy. Down to the schooling arena, where I put her through her paces, performed circles and turns and transitions to get her body supple, her mind active and aware and concentrating on me, to get her balanced, comfortably on the bit. And it all worked like a charm; anyone watching would have thought: that's a guy who knows what he's doing, and he's riding a horse that's been properly schooled.

Five minutes before our round, I took her into the collecting ring, and kept her moving: she hated to be still at such a time. And at once, I felt there was something slightly unusual. I couldn't put my finger on it. There was a certain lightness in my hand: a certain absence in front of me. Hard to describe, but it was as if her head wasn't really there.

I wasn't getting the messages I should have done through my hands. I squeezed harder with my legs, trying to push her onto the bit, trying to get her to engage. I didn't really get anywhere. Still, she was such a quirky mare, it was probably just some new tic she had invented. We'd be all right. We always were.

One minute. Nerves stabbed at me like a red-hot poker in the guts. The familiar doubts assailed me. I dealt with them in the usual way, knowing that once the go came, everything would change. I turned her away from the start, trotted a circle, took up a lot more contact on the reins than usual, trying to counteract this airiness, this unnatural lightness, this no-head feeling. Then, at the very last, turned her to face the first fence.

Go.

I squeezed, expecting that sudden ferocious tug on my arms, ready to throw my weight over her withers, to engage with the jump as one being and take wing.

Nothing.

It was like holding a ghost. Nothing at all: the spookiest thing I have ever felt on a horse. And then, very slowly, very carefully, with finicky, almost pedantic deliberation, she stood on her hind legs. And stayed there. Impossibly balanced on the brink of disaster. And then, after a long, long time, perhaps almost a minute, and almost as slowly, she came down again.

We'd soon put that right.

First problem was to get my left stirrup leather back onto the saddle: a safety device had been triggered while we were up in the air. Someone, perhaps the starter, grabbed the reins and trotted us towards the first fence – flying start, that'd do it, kick kick, one two three and –

We surveyed the course from our lofty eminence, both our heads higher than everyone else's, both of us miraculously in balance. She wouldn't, she couldn't do it. It was all too much. It was all impossible. It was the end.

An amigo too few

We walked back to the stables. It was hard to process what had happened; it was as if the earth has ceased to be solid beneath my feet. But my mind was full not of problems but solutions. Of course we could crack it. Of course it was a temporary aberration. I took her saddle off, made much of her, told her she was great. I left her in her box for half an hour to think things through. Then I put her bridle back on and walked her for a while, in and out of the horseboxes, past the competitors, listening to the tannoy's boom: all the things that can get a horse overexcited. She was fine. She was completely relaxed. Nothing worried her. It was going to be all right.

I put her saddle on, for now I was to ride in the team event. I was to ride with a couple of mates from the yard, father and son: one young, ambitious, a trifle full of himself, the other gentle-mannered and pleased to be having adventures with his son. Nice people. We were listed in the event as The Three Amigos. And I was convinced it would work: that, given two horses to follow, she would set off after them and all would be forgotten. Not a stupid hope: with the herd instinct running strong, reluctant jumpers will often follow a lead horse and take on any fence you care to put in front of them.

We circled together, we amigos. You lead, I said. I'll follow. One minute. Then came the go.

And then we were up in the air again, the two of us, standing so tall you'd think it impossible she didn't fall. I stayed on, but then she wasn't trying to get rid of me. It was just that when I asked to go forward, the signal I gave her made her go up instead of along, and so we stood there, in high perplexity, while the world went on all around us down below. It was as if the wiring of her brain had become unhinged, the right signal bringing a hopelessly wrong response.

She came down again, we tried to start again, we stood up again. And then again. The starter, rightly, had had enough, and he told us to clear off. "One more try," I begged, and it was grudgingly allowed. "You want to ride the course, ride the course," I said to the amigos. "Just go. We'll either follow or we won't."

They went, to complete the course and be disqualified for losing one of their number. We stayed; still and utterly perplexed, we stood. I was left alone, on a horse that stood tall, erect and unable to move forward or back, a horse locked up tight in total bewilderment, with a rider, in dismay, somehow clinging on. The One Amigo.

Unrideable

Over the next few weeks, I tried everything. I rode her in the school: she walked well enough, but as soon as I asked her to move into trot, she stood up. I tried to ride her out, on our old favourite hack: she stood up when we reached the gate. I tried to walk her round her own fields, where the cross-country jumps stood, their competition flags taken down: she stood. Jan tried to help, leading her out, holding fast to the reins, with me on board, but she stood. I rode out a couple of times with some people I knew, but she was so crazy with nerves that it set the others off, dancing and skittering, and, understandably, they didn't care for it. Besides, every now and then, when we had to wait to cross a road, she would stand up, and everyone was terrified in case the habit was infectious. Before long, there was no more ducking it. I was the owner of an unrideable horse.

I'll tell you what you should do

One thing you need never go short of in the horsey life is advice. You have a problem, everyone you know will have the solution. As in most other walks of life, we can solve everybody's problems but our own, but this truth has an added intensity in the horsey life. That's because horses are ultimately unknowable. Everyone always seeks someone who might know better, who might be able to know what the horse is thinking: what can, in fact, never be known.

As a result, in a world in which no one can ever be totally sure, there are a million gurus, wise men, wise women, know-alls, geniuses, whisperers and what-have-you. Some have a worldwide reputation; others may influence only a couple of people at the same yard. But in a world in which most of us doubt ourselves, anyone who offers certainty will get listened to.

And so I had a raft of advice. It seemed that everyone I knew had an idea of how to cure a rearer: a certainty that admittedly stopped short of practical experience. I was struggling for an answer: surely it lay in the deeper knowledge, the longer experience of my horsey friends.

Clonk her on the head with a butt end of a whip when she goes up. No, burst a bag of cold water over her head. No, make that warm water, then she'll think it's her own blood. No, crack an egg on her head, that'll do it. Leap off and pull her over backwards: that'll sort her out. Admittedly, it might break her back, but either she's a ride-able horse or she's a dead horse, so what difference does it make?

It's true that performing the trick of the leaping and the pulling might break my own back or bring the horse down on top of me, but what's life without a few risks, especially if someone else is taking them? A friend of mine rode her when I wasn't at the yard: a generous and brave thing to do. He said that she would walk, trot and canter if you beat her, but there was really no point in trying that again – all I'd end up with was a sour, bitter, beaten animal. Most people suggested I take her to the yard owned by the local farrier. He did a lot of work with problem horses; his wife would ride her and beat some sense into her.

I was seriously considering this last option when I had an idea all by myself.

The answer

I went through a lot of thinking at this time. Why had it all gone wrong? Was it my fault? Was it somebody else's fault? And what could be done to make things better? I wondered if it was my periodic absences, when I was travelling for work, that had confused her, made her uncertain, a horse that lacked a clear rhythm to her life. I wondered if I was riding her wrong; perhaps I gave her too much fun, too much hacking, not enough schooling. I heard that the girl who had kindly ridden her for me while I was away had given her a beating: she had tried to make Dolores walk in a place where she always galloped, and had punished each skip and hop and lunge with a blow of the whip, no doubt believing she was doing me a favour, and helping me with a horse that wanted too much of her own way. That would have added to her confusion: made her think that a galloping place was now full of all kinds of threatening implications. But all of these can only have been contributory factors.

The fact is that now, many years later, I know exactly

what went wrong. I could have stopped things going wrong long before we reached the acute phase. It is amazing that of all the advice-givers, not one was on the right track. It is stone-cold obvious now: and I've no doubt many of my readers have already been shouting the answer at the unresponding pages.

Feed! When you have a problem with overexcited behaviour, the problem is almost always feed. And Jan, with her generous ways, was simply giving Dolores more high-protein food than she could cope with. Like children at a party on a sugar-high, the energy has to go somewhere. At a party, you end up with jelly on the ceiling; with horses, you end up with bolters, buckers, dancers and sometimes, with rearers.

I should have cut down the feed the instant I felt her getting above herself, the instant I felt that she was losing control of her own responses. But I just didn't know enough. It would be years before I understood this. As it was, the problem built up, and I ended up with a lethally dangerous horse: a horse that could not be ridden. And increasingly, the advice I was given was the same. As one adviser put it carefully: "You need to correct the lead shortage in her brain." In other words, shoot her.

It was the only answer.

Sentiment and sentimentality

There are those who think horsey people are all horribly and gooily sentimental about our animals; we call them daft names (like Dolores), treat them with absurd softness and give them kindness that would be better spent on a needy human. There are others who think we are all uncaring brutes who hit our horses with venomous enthusiasm and then kill them as soon as their existence becomes inconvenient.

But the horsey world is vast and generalisations about sentimentality and brutality simply don't work. You can find every type of person around horses, every kind of philosophy about the way the contract between horse and human ought to work. For example, I used to write a column for *Horse & Hound* magazine. I once had lunch with the then editor, Arnold Garvey, who wanted my column to change completely. He wanted me to take up hunting, and write about how much I loved it. In short, he wanted me to write about his vision of the horsey world, not mine.

As lunch wore on, it was clear he was a man obsessed

by death. He talked about death from starters to coffee. He told me about the best way to kill horses, the best time to do so, the best people to do the deed. He talked about the fools who thought that killing foxes was a bad idea. Killing stags was also a good idea, if I but knew it. In fact, killing stuff in general was a good thing. There were too many horses around: that was the key issue. People kept horses when they no longer worked, and there was simply no point at all in a horse unless it was working: i.e. doing something for a human.

He defined this in a narrow way: a horse had to be hard-ridden, supplying some clearly designated, preferably sporting function. Basically, horses either hunted or competed. There wasn't much point in horses apart from that, was there? When a horse got too old or too injured to work, you killed it, simple as that. The hunt people would do it. They always give the horse an apple before pulling the trigger, which shows how much they care. As for those charities that looked after retired horses: that was the worst thing of all. It was a denial of the very reason we keep horses. All these horses should be killed, it was obvious.

I never did write the hunting column. I never wrote for the magazine again, since future participation depended on hunting, and I choose not to hunt. That's my decision, and let's not, for God's sake, go into the debate here. Right now, we're talking about killing horses not foxes.

At every livery yard in the country, you will find at least one, and maybe several people who are soppy to the point of daftness about their horses. They bring them presents, groom them for hours, talk to them in a special silly voice. And you know, that's fine by me, so far as it goes. Wouldn't do if we were all made the same. The soppiest horsey person I ever knew was a woman who worked in catering. Every day, she would come to the yard and bring a catering pack of carrots en julienne. Even on days she couldn't ride, she would pay a visit, just so that she could pass on the carrots and make much of her horse, calling him the cutest little nicknames. Frequently, she brought him cake, which he ate with great good temper. No day was complete without lots of little kisses on her horse's big nose. It wasn't quite decent, but there you go. Her life, her horse. She probably thought I was brutally hard on Dolores.

Then her horse got injured. It was serious and incurable, but not life-threatening. I forget the details, but the upshot was that after a couple of months of box-rest, the horse would be sound enough to hack out again. But it would be no good as a competition horse any more. So the next week, she had the horse killed. She needed the insurance money if she was to buy another competition horse, you see. I'm not sure what the moral of that story is: I'm not even sure that there is one. It's just that the proximity of extreme sentimentality and total ruthlessness made my head swim.

Sentimentality has been called "the unearned emotion". The comedian Russell Brand is keen on that idea. You can also find the same notion in *Ulysses*: Stephen sends a telegram to Buck Mulligan: "The sentimentalist is he who would enjoy without incurring the immense debtorship for a thing done." Sentimentality is a form of self-indulgence, going daft over fluffy little chicks before dining on chicken tikka masala. It might be described as feeling emotions for the simple pleasure of it: in a way that carries no obligation. However, let us always remember that there is a world of difference between sentiment and sentimentality. You can throw out sentimentality of the cake-and-kissing kind, but that doesn't stop you caring about a horse. Caring deeply.

People love cats or dogs, or horses: and when these animals die, the human knows grief. At such a time, there are always people who will pooh-pooh this grief, and deride it as sentimentality. They will think, even if they don't actually say, that you always knew the cat would die, so it's illogical to be grief-stricken when it happens. (The same argument holds true for grandparents.) The death of someone you love is always a hard thing, whether the death came from a clear sky, or whether it was long anticipated; whether the love was for a human being, or whether it was for a being of another species. There is a hierarchy of grief: we feel it more distantly for casual acquaintances, more intensely for those who have played a significant part in our lives. We can feel grief for people we have never met: a writer, for example, who changed our world-view, a musician who brought special joy. We can certainly feel grief for animals. To lose a cat or a horse is not the same as being widowed, but it is not the same as nothing. It's to do with love. It is, in short, an earned emotion.

All horse people have different ideas of what the contract between horse and human involves, and I am not lay-ing out the right and wrong way to draw up such a contract. It is, again, a decision for each individual. The question of killing a horse is one of those little frontier moments that every horsey person must work out for himself. The ultimate truth of the matter is that a human has the power of life and death over his horse, and there comes a time when he must use that power.

Life

I chose life. He swaggered out of his box, disseminating all around him a sense of his own worth. He was a thorough-bred, standing 15.2, just an inch bigger than Dolores, but he carried himself as if he was twenty hands. He was glowing with his own power and beauty. He was called Sykes. He was so full of cock-certainty that he had gone far beyond conceit: he was simply accustomed to the routine of admiration. In the dimness of the barn, he seemed to have a light within: outside in the yard, where he was stood to attention for our admiration, he did the sun a favour by letting it shine on him. He was perfect. You could, if you like, call it love at first sight.

"Don't decide now. Call me when you've thought about it."

Cind and I had already thought about it, but we went away, just for the look of the thing. A couple of days later, I made the call. "And when would you like to bring your mare?" A tryst was arranged.

Love and so forth

So Dolores went to visit Sykes. Did she love Sykes? Silly question, obviously: the two met only for foreplay and coupling, and the first time got her in foal. She always loved male company. O'Malley, being a gelding, had certain limitations, but she was sublimely responsive to Sykes's advances. After it happened, she went out with the broodmares until she was scanned in foal. Then she came back to Jan's to get fat. And of course, once she was back in the field, she teamed up with O'Malley again. As soon as I let her out, there was a great squealing and galloping, and the two were together rubbing noses, then grooming each other, then grazing side by side. They loved to be together, those two: and if O'Malley was incapable of covering a mare, he was more than capable of supplying Dolores with companionship, affection – with love, if you like.

There are things you have to be terribly careful about when you write about animals, and that all counts a thousand times more if you are studying them in a scientific way. No hint of anthropomorphism is permitted. I remember a story of an ethnologist studying baboons. Every time he wrote a word like "friendship" or "companionship", the supervising academic changed it to "proximity". The student responded tartly that perhaps the nearest the professor had got to affection in his own life was proximity.

It is obvious that social mammals have emotional ties to each other: that they enjoy the company of some individuals more than others, miss them when they are gone, feel happy when they are together, actively seek each other out. I have observed that with lions in the Luangwa Valley in Zambia; I have seen it in the horsey fields of England. These ties seem like friendship to me: you could, I suppose, call it love if you wished. It is certainly a meaningful relationship, one that matters to each animal involved, and one that affects their well-being.

All right then: an even more difficult one. Does Dolores love me? You know, I haven't the least idea. Certainly she knows me from other humans. Certainly, she greets me. She has never been a gushing or sentimental mare, but most days, when I see her for the first time, she will give me a gentle bump with her nose: an acknowledgment of some kind of link between us. When I am away for a week or two, she tends to pout: puts her head in the corner of the box and won't come out to talk to me. She rejects proximity, if you prefer. She needs to be talked round: I have, it seems, to be forgiven.

We try and understand non-human animals without anthropomorphisation: but we can only see through human eyes. A horse, we must remember, sees things through a horse's eyes. Dolores feels no academic prohibition against a hippomorphic view of the world. I don't see her as a four-legged human, but I imagine that, at least in some measure, she sees me as a two-legged horse. I know that she trusts me: will let me perform any number of tasks, picking out hooves and grooming and rugging up, without a problem. As a horse and rider combination, we had at times expressed that trust in the most flamboyant fashion. She knows who I am and mostly, she has a good time with me. I am part of her environment, part of her life. That's enough. I really don't ask for more. To expect love from a horse is sentimental, unearned emotion, and the very idea is quite absurdly anthropomorphic.

But we have a bond of some kind, and that is not in doubt. This has been a long and significant relationship for both of us. I am human, so I can acknowledge the love on my part. She is equine: from another world. But we have something, and I am damn sure it's not proximity.

They love!

Cavaliere Ginistrelli was an Italian about Newmarket at the beginning of the last century. He had a mare called Signorina, whom he loved not wisely but too well: in fact, the pair shared sleeping quarters. He arranged a mating for her with one of the top stallions of the town, and led her through the crowded, horsey streets to keep the appointment. At that time, it was the custom for the owners of less sought-out stallions to parade their animals through the streets to advertise their beauty and potency. And on their journey, Ginistrelli and Signorina met just such a low-caste beast called Chaleureux. Federico Tesio, in his classic *Breeding the Racehorse*, takes up the story: "Chaleureux at once proved worthy of his name. He gave signs of a violent infatuation. Signorina looked on him with equal favour and refused to move on. No amount of tugging or pleading had any effect. Ginistrelli sized up the situation at a glance. 'They love!' he exclaimed. 'A love match it shall be.'"

The result of the love match was a filly called Signoretta. In 1908, she won the Derby and then, two days later, the Oaks. She was perhaps the greatest race filly of all time. So naturally, the two horses were given a second chance to express their love. The result was another beautiful filly, this one called Star of Naples. She raced until she was five, and never won a race.

A fire extinguished

I bought a horse because I liked riding horses: now I had made a decision that would leave me without a horse to ride for getting on for two years. That is because a horse's gestation period is eleven months, and a foal cannot be weaned for at least six months. And even after that, there was no guarantee that Dolores would be rideable again. It was all very strange.

I am not trying to strike a moral pose here. Many would have made the decision made by the women with the carrots en julienne: kill the unsatisfactory horse and buy a new one. I didn't make my decision because I am a better person: I made it because I am a different person. For me, it just felt right.

Oh, I had the odd horse to ride, because Jan was forever generous. I paid Dolores a visit every few days; often, Jan would offer me a horse to exercise at the same time, more for my benefit than for the horse. On several occasions, she lent me a horse to compete, partly to see how the horse went, mainly as a favour. I had some pleasant times and always rode back to the yard, told Jan what the horse was like – useful information for a seller of horses – and then went to see my ever-rounder Dolores, give her a groom and a few carrots (not en julienne) and return home. Cind often came with me. She had lost the habit of riding when we returned to England, taken up with a professional life in the theatre, but when it came to the looking-after, rather than the taking of your pleasure, Cind was reinspired with the horsey life.

And me, I had to think things through. I had bought Dolores because I saw myself as a dashing horsey type of chap, forever galloping around the countryside and leaping over ferocious obstacles: brave yet kinda sensitive. I was a man who liked to ride horses, but now, having taken the decision not to ride horses, I had to see myself as something different. I was a man who liked horses. Or rather, a man who liked a horse. I found that there was something in the horsey life beyond action and danger and taking wing. There was my ever-fatter mare, her eyes turned gentle by the lack of stress in her life, and also, I am sure, by some under-standing of the processes that were going on within her. My ball of fire had turned soft and placid: the perplexity and terror she had shown that day at the cross-country start seemed like another time, and another animal. And I, a person who had sought some kind of thrilling conveyance, some passport to excitement, now found myself seeking out motherhood.

A nose and a foreleg

The sound of rattling coffee cups has a Proustian effect on me, instantly catapulting me back in time to the last days of Dolores's pregnancy. That is because for some weeks, every morning, Cind and I would get up and go straight into the car and drive to Jan's yard: in the back, a cardboard box containing the chattering mugs and a thermos. We would arrive, look over the door of Dolores's box and remark: "Only one! Only one horse!" Then we would groom her, feed her carrots, make much of her, and drink coffee. Every evening, we would return, and find her as calm and tranquil as ever, looking quite unlike a horse about to give birth.

The vet had given us good advice, said that the box was a little too small to be ideal as a foaling box, that this is what ought to happen, and that if it didn't, we were to call him. I tried to take it all in. If two back legs came out first, that was fine. If a foreleg and nose emerged at the same time, that was good, too, the best. But if there were two forelegs, that was bad: the foal could not be expelled in such a position because the head would stop it coming. You can tell a foreleg from a hind because the foreleg flexes back and the hind leg forward. Had I got that? Yes, I had. At least I thought I had.

And so, after the evening visit, Cind and I would sometimes stop at a pub, sometimes for a meal. And as things moved on, we started to make a visit to the yard after the pub as well: only to find Dolores blinking as we turned the light on, munching her hay, looking like the calmest creature that had ever been foaled.

Alive and kicking

A strange thing happened, like nothing I had known before. I was tuned into her: I knew exactly what was going on. I had no experience whatsoever of what lay ahead, but at the same time, I had a strange foreknowledge of the process. Perhaps it was the operation of the horsey gene, some atavistic connection with horses. Some would suggest it was a previous-life experience. I don't go in for such things myself, in a general way; all I know was that, at that very strange time, I felt like a stud groom who knew what he was about, knew his stock and knew their ways. I did not presume on this feeling, for I knew I was genuinely ignorant. But all the same: well, I knew. I don't know what it was that I knew, but I am sure I knew something.

I knew, for example, that she would not be dropping the foal any time soon. The weather had turned suddenly chilly. At these big times, the deepest instincts of a horse cut in. A mare wants conditions to be as good as possible for her fragile newborn. So when the weather gets cold, she holds on a little longer. I didn't need to be told this. It was a strange thing, but I knew. I could sense that she was in no itching hurry to let go.

Of course, we still made our regular visits, three times a day, but I was pretty certain that there would be no foal at the end of each one. And I was right. But then the weather changed again; so did Dolores, and so did I. I don't go in for spooky knowledge as a general thing, I won't tell you your sun sign or pull out the tarot cards. But for once, I really did know. It was the most curious feeling. I felt like the fount of all knowledge, even though there was only one thing I knew, and I could hardly be confident that these strange feelings were actually right. I laid my hand on her neck, and read subtle signs of an increased excitement, an increased readiness. "It won't be tonight," I told Cind.

"We'd better check anyway."

"Of course."

So we had supper at a pub and then went back in the dark, and there was Dolores, big and round and wondering, warm to the touch, but calm and still. Not tonight.

The following morning, coffee cups rattling, we drove to Jan's yard. Only one horse in the box, still only one. We drank coffee, made much, saw to hay and water, went home. "It'll be tonight." Naturally at night. Horses almost always drop at night; it's when they are comfortable about the business. Harder for a predator to steal a newborn foal at night.

Early evening: she was restless, warm, even a trace of damp about her neck. Oh yes, tonight. No question. But not immediately. Eat first. So we did. I remember the meal, big, flat, black field mushrooms with stilton melted on them; coarse, tasty, washed down with cold beer. Just what a good midwife needs.

The yard was dark; as ever in a stable-yard, the silence was incomplete: horses fidgeting in their boxes and eating their hay. On with the lights: and there was Dolores in a lather, stomping around the box with dread and purpose in every line of her. This was it all right.

The birth of a foal is a big, dramatic business. It fills the place. The horse is a huge thing and when impelled by an unbearable restlessness, difficult and dangerous. I knew she'd had a foal in a previous life of her own, and was glad to think that she'd know what she was about. That made one of us. She got up, she got down. She stamped another circuit of the box: the foal within her struggling to be born. Sweat covered her, as if we had finished the craziest of gallops.

She got down, a convulsion. Got up again, and made another thundering circle of the box, the forces inside her unbearable. We were outside, watching, not getting in the way. In those days before mobile phones, Cind was ready to drive to a phone box the instant we decided we needed the vet, we couldn't cope, it was all going wrong. Dolores turned: and there was something. I opened the door, stroked her neck, said soft things to her; she stood still, though it cost her an effort. And Cind saw and then I saw the beginning of the day's miracle: a nose and a foreleg.

We retreated; she was down again. The box was not really big enough, I could see that now, and she didn't have

147

the geometrical sense to lie diagonally. She was too close to the wall. I opened the stable door again and this time left it open: and she made a huge sudden dramatic effort. There before me, half a miracle, a foal half-born. And a sudden pause. The foal was stuck between the wall and the mare, half in, half out. Dolores clearly thought she had done enough, was wondering about the next stage. She looked about waiting for a cue. There was a moment of slightly farcical bewilderment.

It was then that I, the world's least practical person, delivered a live foal. I was on my heels behind Dolores, so I put my arms around the wet bloody bundle, and I gave a small tug, starting gently and then increasing the pull. And all at once it happened and I was sitting on my arse with a foal in my lap, soft hooves flailing, busting out of its plastic bag, snorting the amniotic fluid from its nostrils and breathing a strange new thing called air. Time stopped.

I had the vantage point of all vantage points. Call it foal's eye view. And Dolores turned her head and looked to see what had happened, and an expression I had never in my life seen before filled her face: the most extraordinary softening of the eye. It was accompanied by a soft, throaty whicker: a little like the calls that greet the feed trolley, but infinitely gentler, softer, deeper. If this wasn't love, then I have never in my life known love.

Is this love, is this love?

Would you deny her love? Would you say that the reaction of Dolores to her new foal was not love, only an animal instinct? That she was simply responding to a hard-wired piece of biology designed to ensure the survival of her genes? If so, you may have a point, but you must put human mothers into the same category. If you claim that love is only applicable to humans, you must demonstrate that it requires uniquely human attributes: that love requires knowledge, language, intelligence, self-awareness, consciousness. A human mother does not meet her newborn baby until the moment of birth, but if you deny that, then you must deny that love exists at all.

A human mother's love for a newborn human is tied up with the drama of birth after the long experience of the pregnancy: a process of growing awareness of a being within slowly preparing itself for a separate existence. It comes with the certainty that the new being will require a great deal of time and commitment and care and sacrifice. Don't tell me that it's not the same with a horse.

You can make a reductionist case and say that what a horse feels – if the horse feels anything at all – is merely a reward, something that prompts her to take care of the gene-bearing being presented before her. If a female mammal mother wasn't rewarded with warm, gratifying maternal feelings, she wouldn't do the looking-after bit: the feeding with milk from her body that is the great mammalian invention. But if you view it from a purely biological point of view, you must include the human mother within the same complex.

It is pointless to deny that our fellow-mammals feel pleasure and pain. We can see a dog's pleasure in greeting his owners, a cat's pleasure in his own comfort. We can see a horse's pleasure in feed, in violent exercise, in equine company. The only reason for denying such obvious things is that the more we deny that non-humans animals are like us, the more we can exploit them in comfort.

Horses feel pain and pleasure, and so do humans. Horses have complex emotions, and so do humans. For a horseperson, understanding this point is not just a matter of interest but a matter of survival. Horsepeople do not deny that a horse has anger, fear, pleasure, exuberance, excitement, because to do so would be physically dangerous for the human: the reading of mood is an essential horsemanly skill. If we allow so much to horses – and we must – then we can't deny them love. It would be wilfully perverse to deny a mare her love for her newborn foal.

A mare's mother-love is not the same thing in every way as a woman's mother-love. Let's not go over the top here. A horse's love has no words, probably no very clear picture of the future, certainly no feeling that this is an endeavour shared with a life partner. But without this love, no foal is raised. I do not say that horses are four-legged humans: but I do say that there is more in common between humans and horses – between humans and other mammals – than we choose to believe. There is not just a community of physiognomy, but also of community of emotion. If you deny this, you deny the bleeding obvious. And you weren't there, that night in the stable.

Miracle

Dolores got to her feet and licked him dry. I had already observed that it was a colt we had. Even when she had finished, he was still wet behind the ears, so there's another bit of horsey language for you. Then, amazingly, legs all over the place, the little colt staggered to his feet, looking quite alarmingly like a giant spider, with the wild angles of his uncontrollable limbs. He stared around in total bewilderment, and then crashed to the floor like a puppet whose strings had been cut. No good? Not a survivor? With an effort, we kept our nerve a little longer.

Cind drove off to try and beg some boiling water from somewhere to make a bran mash: recommended meal for a mare who has just given birth. I stayed there and watched, in wonder and dread, pondering on this extraordinary thing that had taken place. Can you really credit it? One moment there was one horse in the box, next moment there were two. Is there anything so utterly remarkable in the entire universe?

The foal was too still. It lay in a corner, limbs everywhere, as if it had already had too much. Dolores turned to me and gave me a soft biff of her nose: it seemed like an urgent request for bran mash. There was a silence that continued for maybe half an hour. And then, all once, the colt was on his feet, suddenly finding strength and purpose, as if his puppeteer had just woken up. He walked with tottering but astonishingly accurate steps to his mother, to her back end, and then he inserted his head up between the legs. Butting like a billy goat, he took his first drink: a moment of astonishing violence, of utter determination to live. Dolores took this in remarkably good part.

And then Cind was back, and Dolores was eating her mash, and it was time to get a few hours' sleep. A miracle indeed: and yet it is the most fundamental fact of life, something that happens, in one form or another, to every living thing on the planet. That's why it is a miracle. First one being, then two.

Name

A horse's name should have something of the sire, and something of the dam. The billionaire Paul Mellon, when aged 92, bought a foal by Seeking the Gold out of You'll Be Surprised (i.e. the father was Seeking the Gold and the mother You'll Be Surprised). He called it Wait for the Will. But a horse also needs a good stable name: you can't go, say, Morning, Wait for the Will, old son, have a carrot. Will is OK, though.

Some people have a genius for names. I know of a foal who was born on election night, 1997 and called Landslide; the same lady had a dog called Havoc. I have never quite had the same happy knack, but I did my best. Had the foal been a filly, I had the perfect name. By Sykes out of Alive and Kicking: Nancy Lives, what else? And Nancy is a very agreeable stable name.

But we had a colt. At first I wanted to call him after an assassin-footballer, to get in both the villainy of Sikes in *Oliver Twist* and the kicking part of Dolores's pedigree name. But Norman Bite-yer-leg didn't have the right ring. I quite liked Claudio Gentile, for the great Italian stopper, but I knew I would get fed up with hearing it pronounced like the word for a non-Jew.

So I went for Bullseye, the name of Sikes's dog, and it would give a stable name of Bully, as in friend or mate, as in Blow the Man Down, Bullies. It would mean that I could call him bully-monster, as Trinculo called Caliban in *The Tempest*. All well and good: but when we registered the name in the Non-Thoroughbred Register, Alive and Kicking was rejected, no doubt because all healthy foals are born Alive and Kicking, and the name has already been used far too often. So Cind filled out the new form and gave the dam's name as Dolly Dolores, and when the confirmation came back, she was registered, a trifle unexpectedly, as Dolly Dolores VII. Can there really have been six more like her?

Making a horse

At first, when learning to ride in Hong Kong, the fundamental principle of the teaching was not to spoil the horse: not to make him any worse. When I was riding Favour, she was the one doing the teaching. A horse like that is usually referred to as a schoolmaster; mistress more appropriate in Favour's case. She did the job perfectly. But it was a great adventure when I took on Fairy Fun, aka Trevor, because I had to teach him. It was my job to improve him. He had never jumped, never worked in a school. But at least the basics were there: he knew how to walk, trot and canter, in a rough and ready way; he knew that a kick meant forward and that a pull meant stop; he knew how to go left and right. He was used to being handled by humans on the ground; he was used to humans sitting on top of him. This was by no means a blank canvas.

But Bullseye knew nothing. That was the dizzying thought. He didn't know how to be led, how to be tied up, how to stand still. He didn't have any concept of manners. He had absolutely no idea of what a horse was supposed to do, what a horse was supposed to be, if he was to live a successful and happy life in partnership with humans. He was a nice-looking little thing: he had his mother's bright bay coat, and a similar white star, placed a trifle off-centre, not a Bullseye at all. Right from the start, he look big.

Touch him. That was the thing. Literally from the moment of birth, Bullseye had human hands on him. Dolores accepted my presence around her: not all mares will, they become overprotective, "foal-proud" and will try and see off human visitors with hard expressions and hard teeth. But Dolores allowed me in amongst it all from the first day, and I could go into her box and make much of the foal, and teach him the most important thing he would ever learn: that human beings were on his side, that being with humans was a comfortable place to be.

There was a slight sense of power in the knowledge that I could do irreparable harm with just a moment of tactless handling; fear, too. There was a sense that the grown-up horse would be a reflection of me: also, the feeling that, whatever I did, the horse's own nature would dictate the course of his life. Nature and nurture; as true for a horse as for a human. Well, Dolores was doing her part all right: looking after him solicitously in the box, feeding him, giving him a sharp correction when he stepped out of line and behaved in a manner she found unacceptable. The first disciplinary lessons of a horse, or of any domesticated animal, are taught by the mother.

So I got Bullseye to wear a foal slip, a foal's head collar, and got him to accept that walking to and from his field with a human was a good thing. Foals will follow their mothers, so the process isn't essential, but the earlier you start getting a horse accustomed to humans, the easier it is for everybody.

Sometimes he would run, sometimes buck, sometimes try and spin round and kick out, so it took a bit of tact and awareness. A hand on the bum helped, too: that little body can turn in an instant of time – a foal's reactions are much sharper than those of a fully grown horse for the excellent reason that the instructions from the brain have less distance to travel. With a foal, a handler has to learn a different rhythm.

But we began to find problems once we got to the field. Jan had organised things beautifully, with a nice field where Dolores and the foal could run together. But after a few weeks, Dolores began to find this situation difficult. She started running up and down the fence line calling to the other horses. She felt alone, isolated, agitated. She was constantly in a sweat and dither. This was not good for her or the foal. Something had to be done.

Personal space

A horse without manners is no horse. Manners makyth horse all right: without manners, a horse can't so much as stay alive. A horse – like a human – must be trusted to behave in certain ways. A good horse will run on the tramlines of his good manners: accept the conventions of decent behaviour unthinkingly, behave in a way that can be predicted. Good manners are the structure on which any society is built: the human-horse co-operative is not an exception. Children are taught to say please and thank you and to be quiet at times when noise is inappropriate, to eat food without hurling it around the room and to accede to the reasonable requests of an adult. Dogs are taught not to jump up at people, not to beg for food at the table, not to sit on the furniture (at least not when anyone is looking). And horses have their own suite of required standards of behaviour. We call it manners, and it is not an entirely anthropomorphic notion. If the idea seems to imply that the contract between humans and horses is a two-way thing, understood by both parties, perhaps that really is the way it is.

Good manners are primarily about a horse's relationship to a human on the ground. The horse must tie up and stand still. He must not shift about, chucking his head around, stamp his feet, fidget or strop. He must accept the fact of being tacked up. He must lift his feet to be picked out. He mustn't pull away when he is being led, or spook, or crowd his handler. He must walk when a human leading him walks, stop when the human stops. Above all, he must respect the personal space of any human being. In other words, he must learn to behave unnaturally: almost as a conscious effort.

Horse are huge. If they lack manners, they are utterly overwhelming. I have spent a little time with Suffolk punches, the giant chestnut heavy horses that used to till the land in Suffolk. To tell the truth, I have always found them slightly alarming. They are so big that humans seem truly insignificant to them. Their concept of their own personal space is very well developed, and it is nothing to them to ease a human out of the way. To compensate for this, a handler must be strong and assertive, but not loud and bullying, because they don't like that either. It is vital for the handler to get through the slightly dim, don't-know-your-own-strength attitude of this amiable giant. It's about tact: but then everything with horses always is.

I used to have a lot to do with a young horse that had been hand-reared by two very gentle ladies. The horse had no manners at all. For him, the boundaries between the two species were unclear, and his sense of his own limitations was fluid. The ladies' arms always carried a rainbow of marks from playful nips the horse gave them. I don't want to come over as the great horseman here, but I had comparatively little trouble with the horse. With me at least, he learned the rudiments of good manners. I used my elbows, my voice, above all my body language, to tell him that I was dominant over him, and that I required respect. If he was in the mood to climb playfully all over me – and he generally was – I would try and stop it before it started. A tug on the lead rope, a don't-even-think-about-it growl, an elbow into the neck: and he would at once remember I wasn't a nice lady. He tried to bite me many times; every time, I would try and meet his lunge with an elbow in the teeth. That may sound a little extreme. Certainly, it sometimes caused me pain when I caught it wrong. But he didn't bite me. We established an effective relationship and I got him to work quite nicely. The fact is that horses who think they can bite humans any time they feel like it are not horses anybody wants to have around. A horse that can't be taught manners is a dead horse.

That has to be the case, if you think about it. A horse that bites, kicks, savages his handlers and breaks away from where he is tethered is not something most people are prepared to put up with. It's too dangerous: a human will end up injured or dead. That is why, over the millennia, humans have bred from horses that are amenable to the teaching of manners.

It's the deal. A horse cannot be part of human life unless he is prepared to concede a certain amount of ground. This is not about the creation of robots: humans love a certain amount of wildness in their horses, actively seek the expression of individuality, and relish any personal quirks. Dolores had a million of them, and many would consider her habit of walking off before I was properly in the saddle a classic example of bad manners, something that should be urgently schooled out of her. I made the decision to ignore it, because it didn't bother me. And besides, she was never any problem when I was on the ground. She was always the sweetest and meekest thing you could wish to meet.

Manners, then, are the biggest area of compromise for a horse. He must accept that a human's decision is final, and that a human's personal space is sacrosanct. The best way of teaching a horse this is by good handling when he is young. You must not be loud and obstreperous, nor must you be a pushover. Like so many other things in the horsey life, it comes down to the kind of person you happen to be.

Moving

It seemed clear that Dolores needed company; that being on her own with her foal was not enough for her. In truth, I know now that feed was also very much a part of the problem: Jan's generous ways were too much for Dolores. I wish I had known then that she had too much fuel to burn, and it was making her stressed: up and down the fence she ran, calling piteously, a picture of unhappiness. Something had to be done, so we looked for a place where she could run with mares and foals, or at least with young stock, and, when we found a yard that promised just that, we moved. There were no bad feelings; Jan drove me and the horses in her lorry, and we moved in. It was all right. True, the mare and foals never materialised, not the last strange incident at that yard, but Dolores and Bullseye settled in very agreeably. The yard was less frenetic than Jan's without the comings and goings and the constant changes of equine personnel. They got the feeding right, too. Dolores relaxed into a calm, maternal trance, and the foal prospered and grew, and carried on growing. It was clear that he was going to be a whopper. And me, I began to wonder about the surrounding countryside. What was it like for riding?

Fait accompli

Bullseye was just over six months when Cind and I went away for the weekend. We came back the following Monday to find that he had been weaned. The women who ran the yard decided between them that it was time to do it, so they did it unilaterally. They chose the old-fashioned, traumatic method: they simply took Bullseye away from his mother and locked him up in a box with the top door closed and let him squeal his head off and kick his heart out against the door. This was not what we had been planning, but there it was: a fait accompli. Livery yards, as I have said, tend to be extremely odd places. This place turned out to be odder than most. I don't think Bullseye ever trusted humans 100 per cent after that.

Sunday service

Sunday morning before eight o'clock is a secret place. It is the domain of madmen and rebels. If you go there, you find such people without difficulty, most of them running or cycling, a few of them walking with dogs. It is a place where you can get away from other humans: but oddly, most of the people who go there exchange a merry greeting with each other. We are creatures of the same kind: co-conspirators. The road outside the yard was for once silent.

She had stood perfectly quiet as I tacked her up. I affected a body language of the utmost nonchalance, a sort of Marcel Marceau mime of an unworried man, at the same time willing my heart and my breath to slow down. This was at best a partial success. I placed my left foot in the left iron: and we were off, precisely as usual, marching off incontinently as I swung my leg over her back and settled into the saddle. Worried that if I touched her with my heels, she'd be off, or up. Worried that if I took up too much of a contact, or not enough, she'd be off, or up. Worried that a car would do the same, or a dog, or a flying plastic bag.

We walked along the road, just she and I. There'd been a lot of working up to this. Cind had ridden her first, rightly assuming that my own anxieties would muddle Dolores and add to her stress. But Dolores stood up for her: it was only months afterwards that she told me. A day or so later, I rode her, with immense trepidation. She didn't stand, though I could feel her thinking about it: the same uncanny lightness in front. She moved forward, just about. It was awkward, peculiar; her stride was short and choppy: she'd lost the habit of being ridden and was half thinking about standing up at every stride. It was not much less than two years since I had last sat on her.

I worked her a couple of times in the yard's little indoor school. There was one standing episode, when I really did think that it was all over, and that two years had all been in vain, but with some very sound help on the ground from Janet, one of the women who ran the yard, we got through it. The next time I rode her, she was fine.

So I went for a gradual escalation, and rode her out in company, and here at last she relaxed, and walked out. Next time we trotted; time after that, we even risked some mild canters. It was great: I could feel her regaining confidence, and without a doubt, she could feel me doing the same thing. I was taking everything with the care of a man restoring a Ming vase: hurry was way beyond my budget. But gradually, I got to the point when to delay any longer would have been footling. It was time for the big one. An expedition alone, without the moral support of other horses, just she and I again, just as it used to be. But I needed to shift the odds in my favour as much as possible. I needed a road with no traffic: and I knew I could only find that on a Sunday before breakfast.

I was out for about 45 minutes. We went round the block. We never stepped off the tarmac. We never once went out of walk. There was scarcely a vehicle to deal with. Nothing happened. Nothing whatsoever. I got back, and there was Cind waiting: worried about my safety, worried about the state I'd be in if it had all gone wrong. But nothing did go wrong. We had walked round the block. It was one of the greatest triumphs of my life among horses. I got off her, patted, untacked. It was the tamest, quietest ride I have ever had in my life, and I have ridden cross-country rounds that cost me more. I had staked rather more than I wanted to on this one-horse race, but it seemed I had won. It seemed that I had a horse again.

Glittering prizes

There are a thousand small nuances of snobbery in any livery yard, but the biggest of them is about competition. If you compete, you are a serious person. If you don't, you are just messing about. Someone who competes is by definition more important than someone who doesn't. A competitor has goals. A competitor works in the school with a serious face. A competitor is ever-so-slightly patronising to those who don't compete. Of course, a good few of these serious competitive types seldom actually turn out at competitions. They are always just about to peak and gain the rewards of all their hard work, or they are working on a small weakness and as soon as it is eliminated, they will start gathering the prizes they have been working for.

It is a rum notion, that to be serious about horses you have to take part in competitive sport. What's more, it's an idea that takes no account of the facts. Many horsey people find complete fulfilment in their horses without going near a competition: but because of the prevailing snobberies, they feel the need to apologise for this oversight, or to disguise it by working for competitions they never enter. There is a term for non-competitive horsey types: happy hacker. It is an insult.

Well, I was full of hopes for getting Dolores back on track as a happy hacking horse, and I had no intention whatsoever of competing on her. It would be too stressful for her, and no doubt for me as well: and it might bring back the nightmare. In other words, I had made a decision to become a happy hacker. I was content with the second part, and since the first part is one of the great goals of humankind, I thought I could probably live with it. And perhaps I would end up competing with Bullseye.

I had had great fun competing. What I liked best about it was that it gave a structure to my horsey life. With my Hong Kong horses, this involved a lot of schooling: first to teach me to jump, latterly to teach Trevor to jump. This was one of the great adventures, and Trevor's ability in show-jumping – smooth, confident, athletic – was as gratifying a thing as I have ever known. With Dolores, there was nothing to teach. It was a question of fitness and rhythm. We had some marvellous times competing – and yet I never really felt that competition was necessary.

You find a lot of people at livery yards who really enjoy schooling a horse. That is to say, trotting round and round in circles. There is a fascination to be found in schooling, that's undeniable, and any sort of progress with a horse (or anything else for that matter) is an enthralling thing. It's a fine thing to do for its own sake, but that somehow doesn't seem enough. That's why so many people who love schooling have some mythical competition as their goal: a competition that never quite happens. It's not competition that's essential: it's the idea of competition. If you weren't working up to a competition, you'd have to ask yourself: what's the bloody point? Without a competition, there is no reason for what you are doing: you are just messing about. You might as well be a happy hacker; and who can live with the shame of that?

But the truth of the matter is that there is no point in any of it. There is no point in hacking out, no point in schooling, no point in taking part in competitions. There is no point in horses, none whatsoever. And if there is a point, it is the same for every horsey activity in the world, from happy hacking to racing for a purse of millions. It comes down to one thing and one thing only: some people just happen to like being around horses. We have horses because we like them. We have horses because horses fulfil some strange need in us. That's true for the most elegant of dressage queens, the most precise of showjumpers, the most gung-ho of eventers; and exactly the same thing is true of circlers in the school and the hackers who are merely happy.

And it is something that affects the paid and the unpaid. It is a thread that runs right through the horsey world, from sheikhs to Pony Club children. The same need: the same seeking of fulfilment and happiness by means of the horse.

Hand on the buckle

Foot in the iron, and off she would go. I would swing on board, catching her up as she went on her way, and we were gone. Again. The experiences had not scarred her. She was neither sadder nor wiser than before; and if I was both, I soon forgot it when we were at it again. Her madcap nature had not been moderated by maternity. A walk was still on the edge of a trot, a trot was always begging for a canter, and a canter could become a gallop at the smallest tipping-forward of my weight.

And so we explored the new chunk of country, and found places that suited us. We paid special attention to the places where we could stroll, and to the places where we could gallop. The best of riding is to be found at these two paces: the one so relaxed and easy that the mind wanders off towards some kind of meditative trance, in which nothing matters, nothing much even exists, and everything has been reduced to the interaction of a couple of bodies and a pair of minds. And then the gallop, when your senses are at once at their sharpest, concentration is flicked on like a switch, nothing matters but your balance and the minute shifts of your hands. Your mind achieves a peculiar clarity because, if it didn't, things would go wrong. You are calling on an ancient survival mechanism with every flat-out charge. Both these states of mind, the state of walk and the state of gallop, are joyous things, and for me they add up to one of the compelling attractions of the horsey life. You have the hand-on-the-buckle walk, which is a state of nothingness; and you have the bum-in-the-air gallop, which is a state of everythingness. Or is it the other way round?

No matter. We found our good places, and we refound that old companionship of the roads and the bridleways: that unthinking sympathy, that sense of being fellow-conspirators, always looking together for the next gallop. Back at the yard I would tend to Bullseye and lead him about in hand and teach him the basic truths about being a horse – that is to say, being a domestic animal capable of living with humans, the single necessary attainment for all tame horses. But when that was done, I would be off with Dolores again, teaching her nothing whatsoever. Other way round, as usual.

Hunting the hunters

But I missed out hunting people in my chapter on snobberies. Apologies, then, to hunting people everywhere. How could I forget? Of course, there are also hunting people who think that non-hunting people don't know what they are doing with horses, and that non-hunting horsepeople are just messing about. All horsepeople think that their own way of doing things is the best, if not the only way. Me included.

And me, I don't hunt, as I said. And I'm still not going to debate the rights and wrongs of it. I know and like carnivores and vegetarians, believers and atheists, socialists and Tories: I know and like hunting people and non-hunting people. Make your own mind up.

Jan loved the hunt. A good few people at her yard hunted. "You should come, we never catch a bleedin' fox," Jan said, but I never did. There were no conflicts between hunters and non-hunters at the yard, not even much of a division. We all had horses in common, after all. Just occasionally, there might be a few amiable teases: a suggestion that this way was best, that this horse was best, that this way of living the horsey life was best. So one day, I joined Jan and her hunting pals for a sponsored ride: twenty miles across lovely countryside and a few jumps for those that wanted to jump.

Naturally, the hunters teased me about not hunting, and not knowing what I was doing, and how their horses could canter all day, and how they were the real gung-ho riders. It was all good fun; they were great people, and out for a good day. No trace of rancour whatsoever. All the same, I felt I had a point to make. So we came across a wide, broad expanse, and a cavalry-charge canter was suggested ("Hope it's not too much for you") and off they went. I held Dolores back, and when they looked around to see where we had got to, we were a couple of hundred yards behind. "What's the matter, can't get out of a trot?"

We streaked past them at a flat gallop, my face buried in the mane, and pulled up 200 yards ahead of them. Only Jan was able to live with the pace. Later on, we showed we could do it when there were jumps in the way as well: the hunters took the jumps at an easy all-day canter: Dolores and I completed the course in our customary scalded-cat style. We, I think, had made our point. We made our way back in great good temper with each other; it had indeed been a great day.

The chief teaser handed me his hip-flask. "Little bloody rocket," he said, looking down at my stubby little mare. I took a swig, passed it back; a very nice bloke. It's always best not to make glib judgments, don't you find?

Making a stand

She developed two rather dramatic little quirks. The first invariably came at the cross-country course. For the payment of a subscription, it was possible to ride round two or three miles of country, a ride that contained plenty of jumps. By this time, I had retired Dolores from jumping, following my commitment to stress avoidance. But it was still a marvellous place for a serious and comparatively stress-free burn-up. The only problem was getting in. The entrance was via a hunting gate: that is to say, you opened it with a long lever you could reach from the saddle. But it was tremendously stiff, and Dolores, anticipating the gallop, would always go completely berserk, jumping round and round in circles, so that I couldn't reach the lever long enough to get any purchase on it.

So I had to jump off, hold her reins while she curvetted about, open the gate, which was hard when trying to control a horse who has mislaid her senses, and then close it behind me. That was the easy bit. Getting on was the seriously exciting part. You had to get a foot in the iron, which was hard, since by this time you practically had to scrape her off the ceiling. Generally, this would end up in a kind of mad hopscotch, she on four legs and me on one, going round and round until I could get enough foot on the ground close enough to the horse to swing myself up.

Well, I'm sure you can guess what happened next. As soon as my weight had left the earth, she took off like a drag-racer. My first task was to find the saddle with my arse, the second was to persuade her that I had some kind of stake in the decision-making process, the third was to find the other stirrup iron. It was at such times that I wondered if those people who told me that I must always insist that a horse stands still while being mounted had some kind of point. But eventually, I would catch a bit of iron with my toe, and that would stabilise matters. At the last mile, all uphill, we would give it the lot and eventually pull up, she still in a lather of delight at her own madness, me looking back over the ground we had covered: the smoke still rising from the scorch marks we had left on the turf.

Her other quirk was less sensible. She was fine out on the roads, absolutely fine. The only thing was that whenever we came upon a T-junction, she would stand on her hind legs. It was not a matter of panic, that was the rum thing. It was not even especially dangerous. It was just something she felt she had to do. She would go up slowly, almost apologetically, stay up there a little while, and then get down again in her own good time, and we would proceed. Partly, it was because she could no longer bear to be kept waiting; partly also, I think, it was because she couldn't bear to see the end of a road. I must say, it certainly stopped the traffic: I never had so much courtesy, never so much room. All the same, this behaviour was not to be encouraged.

So I planned my routes carefully, to make sure there was no T-junction, sometimes making absurd detours to avoid these terrible places. She was absolutely fine in every other respect, though waiting did upset her. There was one right turn, I remember, on a road that was sometimes busy, and if she decided to stand up there, life would be seriously problematic. But we pre-empted this. My technique was to take an ultra-bold line down the middle of the road while making an absolutely implacable right-turn signal. They stopped for us all right: we never had a problem.

All was well, then. Bullseye was progressing very nicely. He was great to be with and he already looked quite ridiculously handsome. And me, I would ride my mad little mare across the country and rejoice. The change of yards had worked well. But then the new yard went broke, and we had to move again. I hoped very much that we could find a place without too many T-junctions.

Tail washing

Behind all the snobberies lies the fear. Fear stalks every avenue, every passageway, every stable, every gallop, every school. It is not snobbery that is a constant of horsey life, it is fear. It is not a large thing, it is not a thing you worry about, it is not even a thing you notice terribly much. But it is always there. Generally, it is pretty subtle: a grain of salt in a pint of water. But even for the bravest, even for the most blasé, even for the most confident, even for the most empathetic, even for the most sensible, fear is inescapable.

I don't mean you feel frightened: fearful and trembling, hands quaking, every time you get on a horse. Perish the thought. It's just there, in the background: the knowledge that every ride might be your last. It's a fact of life. Very few of us dwell on it, or are even aware of it. It's something that we are simply used to. Of course, if you do the madder things like riding cross-country, team chasing, point-to-pointing, riding young horses, then you are more aware of it. But mostly, it's the subtle background and it's as much a part of the horsey life as the smell of the muckheap.

At many livery yards, you will meet horsey people whose nerve is shot, but who cannot stop being with horses. Some come to terms with this: others cover it up. I remember a very nice woman who was at the yard all the time she could spare, and she hardly ever rode. She groomed. The horse gleamed. "Your tail's a disgrace," she would say, and the tail would be shampooed, combed out with baby oil, brushed, dried, till it was looking a picture. Then the horse would go out in the field and pick up a hundred burs, or lie down in his box and roll in shit. But that was good, not bad, because it meant that the lady was unable to ride, the tail being once again disgraceful, and she was simply forced to shampoo all over again.

Do I feel contempt for this? None whatsoever. We are all of us only a single ride from losing our nerve, or worse, as I have said. Any way that you enjoy horses without damaging them is all right by me. And she was terribly nice to the horse and to everybody else.

Many others pretend they haven't lost their nerve. You find riders who obsessively school, because they no longer dare to ride out. A friend of mine was giving a course in riding and horsemanship and was constantly challenged by the dominant female of the group. It turned out the woman in question hadn't dared to go out of a trot for three years.

I was frightened at the idea of riding Bullseye. I was also very excited about it, but fear was a part of the excitement. I was always frightened that Dolores would pull one mad trick too many. I didn't lie awake in terror thinking of these things: but they were there: small, subtle, an ineluctable aspect of the horsey life.

But I should add one more story before I finish with this last yard. One afternoon, Dolores and I were riding out. We were crossing a field at a purposeful walk. Dolores then did the most absurd double take. She suddenly noticed that the field had been fenced off with electric tape, and that there were a couple of dozen heifers in there. She gave a ridiculous little jump and half-turn – and I found myself standing to attention at her head. I had come off without even knowing it, and had landed standing up before I had worked out what was going on. I'll swear she looked more than a touch embarrassed as I got back on again. It was the only occasion, in the entire course of our time together, that I came off her.

Et in arcadia ego

There are times when life seems to have been suspended from the normal round; when you are for some reason let off the normal snags and worries that beset us; when you live an idyll; when you scarcely dare to breathe, lest you disturb the perfection of all that surrounds you. Dolores and I had an Indian summer, an Edwardian interlude, a period of perfection, a time when God was in his heaven, and all was right with the world. It was a period in the greenwood, time in the enchanted combe, a short stay in Shangri-La. Et in arcadia ego: yes, just like the chapter in *Brideshead Revisited*: "If it could only be like this always – always summer, always alone, the fruit always ripe and Aloysius in a good temper..."

We had an appropriate backdrop for such thoughts, for we had moved to a livery yard set in the ground of Wrotham Park, a stately home just inside the M25. You would recognise it if you saw it: it is used widely by film-makers. Lady Chatterley and Mellors had their own idyll here; I rode out daily past Mellors's cottage, where he showed her ladyship his novel ideas about flower arrangement. The terrace at the big house is a place that seems incomplete without Bertie Wooster turning up as an impostor while ice formed on the butler's upper slopes, or perhaps it was Psmith, impersonating a poet and signing copies of his alleged masterwork with the words "across the pale parabola of joy".

Dolores and I certainly travelled across the pale parabola of joy at Wrotham Park. The house itself was inspiring enough: a slightly clunky Palladian façade, and it made me feel like an extra in a Stubbs painting every time I rode past. Up the drive, past a couple of fields of post-and-rail; fencing that constrained a group of highly expensive thoroughbred mares, for the Byng family had interests in bloodstock. On through the gates, across a minor road and into a narrow lane, a dead end seldom visited by cars. After a couple of hundred yards, you would enter a complex of half a dozen interlinked fields, all caught up in the set-aside scheme and so out of production. We had permission to ride there: Dolores and I would, of course, canter every step as a matter of personal pride, making the sharp right-angles and u-turns with our usual aplomb, never once breaking stride. There were a few places where we would stretch out, at others, I would check her back and she would respond instantly, glorying in her own virtuosity. Sometimes, we met the player of a French horn, a man who came to the fields to enjoy a spot of al fresco practice, but not as much, I suspect, as his neighbours.

The M25 was in sight for part of the way, and often, we would travel past the enmired cars in our own unstoppable three-quarter time. Every driver and passenger of the becalmed cars looked on enviously as we overtook them, wondering if I was a hundred years behind or about five years ahead.

There were a handful of other livery-owners at the yard, and all very pleasant. We would all stop and exchange views whenever we encountered each other, on foot or on horseback. The only drawback was that sometimes, if conversation went on too long, I'd have to make my excuses and leave. "Sorry, I've got to kick on now, or she'll stand up."

"What?"

And she would. Not that she meant anything by it, not any more. It was a trifle alarming to the other riders until they got used to it, but to me it was nothing. A terrible trauma had become a lovable quirk, one more little expression of her personality, without which she – and I – would be incomplete.

Unusually, there was another male rider at the yard. Jeremy and I would sometimes have pints, and often go out for a gallop. He had a rangy grey mare, three-parts thoroughbred, who was too swift for Dolores and me to catch, but we had a fine time trying. Debi Thomas, who ran the yard, was a dressage rider at Grand Prix level, fabulous to watch as she performed her passage and piaffe and her single tempi changes while I was trying to make a horse walk and trot. Sometime she and I would ride out, she on her champion mare Truday, and me on Dolores. All dressage horses should get out and smell the grass and kick their heels up from time to time, or they get stir-crazy. Debi and I would walk on the buckle, and then have a bit of a burn-up: even at this pace, Truday moved like a queen, while Dolores as always scurried like an urchin.

Oh, it was a rich time, and I was able to walk to the yard from home. I am a non-driver, so this was a wonderful bonus, especially for Cind. By this time, we had started a breeding programme of our own; Joseph spent some early times around the horses and among the bluebells at Wrotham Park. Our house faced a small wood and a sheep field; there was another small chunk of woodland at the back. I could walk along an unpavemented road past the farm to visit my horses. London, twenty minutes away by train, was another universe.

Jonjo

An Irishman called Jonjo helped me to get Bullseye started. He was a nice man with wonderful hands and a soft voice and we made a great beginning to it all. But then a horse, not Bullseye, kicked him in the balls and put him out of action for a week. This turned out to be a wonderful calling of my bluff: I had no option but to carry on where Jonjo had left off. So I did: and found myself coping better than I had feared. It was one of those little personal revelations: I was more like a real horseman with every passing day.

Jonjo recovered and took up the reins again. "I'm grand. But they're still a bit large." A week later, I was riding Bullseye. That's when this enchanted time took a slightly different turn. I now had two horses to ride. I would arrive at the yard, tack up Bullseye and school him very carefully, seeking small advances, taking setbacks in my stride. Every time, before I got onto him, I would have to compose myself, bring down the pulse and respiration as best I could, make my body language calm and confident, and get on and do it. It was something of a performance: I often felt as if I were acting the part of a man being slightly brave: not at all the same thing as being brave yourself.

And then when it was done, I would throw a leg over Dolores and go off hooliganing around the countryside without a care in the bloody world. It was perfect.

Polo mints

It was a frosty day, the ground like iron. The fields were unrideable. The outside world was unrideable. That's if you planned to canter, and we always planned to canter. Besides, the roads weren't safe: the tarmac was skiddy with ice and it's no fun for anyone when a horse falls over. So I opted to ride in the school: the freeze was not deep enough to affect the surface of sand and rubber. I gave Bullseye a quick blast on the lunge, and then got Dolores tacked up. I wondered how long it was since I had last ridden her in a school.

I used to throw in the occasional session when I was at Jan's and we were still competing. I would generally do it before or after a hack: a little formal work, looking for things like suppleness and co-operation. Occasionally, I would pop her over a jump: but jumping thrilled her so much that mostly, we kept it for the great days. I schooled her a fair bit while I was rehabilitating her after the birth of Bullseye, preparing her for life as a happy hacker.

But I have done miles in schools on many other horses. If I had a quid for every ten-metre circle I have ridden,

I'd be a millionaire, that's for sure. The ten-metre circle is the basic manoeuvre of schooling. You look for shape, bend, balance: a simple formal exercise that becomes more fiendishly complicated the more you look for perfection. If you drop in at any livery yard, you will see people trotting round and round in circles, faces locked tight in concentration. And always in trot, for some reason. People love to school in trot: you'd think trot was the only gait that mattered. In fact, any dressage test splits the marks more or less equally between walk, trot and canter; halt is pretty important as well. But most riders feel that trot is the gateway to perfection. Walk is too dull (and quite astonishingly difficult to perfect), while too much canter makes you look a bit of a cowboy, and you wouldn't want that, would you? For some sad souls, canter is too alarming, and to be avoided at all costs. So trot and trot and trot: round and round and round, ten metres and ten metres and then again, ten metres.

I took Dolores into the school and warmed her up carefully, walk and trot, to get her feeling chipper, supple and ready to rumble. So I asked for canter, and we rolled into the best, the most pedantic, the most silly, the most nitpicking canter we were capable of, and cantered about the school for a bit, every now and then changing the rein, that is to say, changing direction. Once we'd got that established, it was time to show off.

Every school contains a series of letters, marking salient points around the oblong. They are arranged in a bizarre and confusing fashion, one that has no logic about it whatsoever. In an eight-letter configuration, the middle of the short sides will carry the letters A and C; one long side will have the sequence, K, E and H, and the other F, B and M. What genius came up with that? And why? But never mind: you have to learn them; they are the basis of every dressage test, and every lesson is full of instructions: "Ten metres circle at A… at B, forward into walk."

So Dolores and I performed a kind of anti-lesson. At every letter, we performed a circle. At canter. And less then five metres in diameter, so that her nose was all but touching her tail. I should point out that this is impossible: the only horses regularly required to perform such manoeuvres are polo ponies. Dolores and I performed these Polo-mint circles at every letter around the school, eight in one direction, and then eight in the other. It was an astonishing performance of gymnastic skill, obedience and willingness, and I had to admit that it was all about the brilliance of the horse, rather than the rider. Still, the rider enjoyed the showing-off part every bit as much as the horse. Then we warmed down, well pleased with ourselves. I noticed that Jeremy was watching with a slightly sardonic expression.

I got Dolores rugged up and in her box, and then Jeremy and I went for a pint. "I was talking with a few others in the tack room," Jeremy said. "We agreed that of all the people at the yard, you have the best relationship with your horse." I was stupid enough to take this as a compliment to myself, but I was eventually to be put right on this score. It was Bullseye that did the putting right, and it was as hard a lesson as I have ever had on a horse.

Bumpkins

I was in a bit of an elegiac mood. I walked to the yard, savouring everything I saw. Summer was more or less gone, autumn more or less begun. Everything seemed strangely precious. This was to be my last ride at Wrotham Park. The park had never looked more lovely, the home more stately, the fields of horses more perfect.

I fished Dolores out from the gang of mares and tacked up. We walked across the park, and out through the wrought-iron gates, down along the lane to the gate into the field system, still gloriously set aside. We rolled into our canter, and didn't miss a stride, every single yard of the hedge-line duly covered in immaculate three-quarter time. We had the place to ourselves. The horn-player was not there. No courting couples. No pairs of cars meeting for shady deals. The M25 hummed away peacefully, a somnolent hum. We skipped, we danced, we did all our usual stuff, and we downshifted from canter to walk in a single stride as we rejoined the road. We walked slowly back, me holding the buckle of the reins. The robins were singing again; the kestrel hovered over the corner of the field. We reached the T-junction and waited for a moment as a couple of cars demanded precedence, but the way became clear even as Dolores lifted her front feet from the ground, so we proceeded without a proper stand. Back through the park. I jumped off Dolores for the last time, gave her a pat and a mint, turned her out.

"I'll be back to collect them both in a couple of weeks," I told Debi. "I've got transport all arranged, and a place at the far end." We were moving to Suffolk. London would no longer be twenty minutes away. The longer the horses had stayed at Wrotham Park, the further London had become. All my time was spent between the house and the horses, plus a bit more in the woods and fields with Joseph, who was now three. His passions were tractors and throwing stones into the stream. London had ceased to be a factor in our lives. It was time to go. The horses would follow. I looked forward to years of riding Dolores around the bridleways of Suffolk, living the country life. It was time.

Home at last

Imagine it. Looking out of the window of your own bedroom and seeing your own horses. It's the most glorious thing in the word. Terrifying, too, because you know they'll die if you don't look after them right. But glorious all the same, absolutely glorious. And there was Dolores, walking about the place as if she owned it, eating grass, the Suffolk sun shining on her bay coat.

Her box was just behind the house, and it had been mucked out by me. The hay had been provided by me. The water had been poured into her bucket by me. The morning feed and the evening feed had been mixed and served by me. Home at last: it was life with Dolores as it always should have been, as I had always wanted it; and, it seemed, as if it had always been.

Oh, it was wonderful to have the horses at home. True, I had to become a new person to cope with it: practical, responsible, and willing to do almost any amount of manual toil. I took it all on willingly, and the sight every morning of the face of Dolores, big ears and white star like

Madagascar, looking over the door, gladdened my heart. And she whickered a greeting to which I would reply in mere words, and the daily business of the horsey life would begin.

It was all splendid; it was all perfect. The snag was that I was unable to ride Dolores. And I would never ride her again. It happened in the couple of weeks between our move to the country and the arrival of the horses. She was mucking about in the field, as horses do, and she had an accident. The Achilles tendon slipped off the point of hock: that is to say, off the sharp elbow-like joint on the back leg. The vet was bullish: "Don't worry, I've known 'em race again after that injury."

But it was not to be. She didn't come sound again, and eventually it was clear that she never would. Well, I had a decision to make. Again. And it was easy. "So long as she gets a kick out of life, she gets a kick out of life." As before, I make no extravagant moral claims for myself. Perhaps I didn't make the decision for her at all. Perhaps I just made it for me.

Irreconcilable differences

In the end, I gave up on Bullseye. It was a question of my own sanity. I have gone over the story a million times in my mind, but here, I'll be brief. He was never happy after we moved. He had a very difficult time at the livery yard, where we kept the horses before we were able to bring them home. He then went to a remedial yard, at vast expense, to have his problems solved: and it was a disaster. Instead of getting better, he got strangles, a respiratory infection, and so he had to go through a prolonged period in isolation. This put into reverse the limited good the yard had done. I eventually collected a horse that was confused, solitary, ignored, morose, at odds with the world. I never quite won his trust back.

In truth, he and I were never compatible. He was a big, strong-minded, self-assertive gelding; he needed to be dominated, reminded that his place in the hierarchy was one place lower than my own. I never quite knew when to back down with him. I never got the timing right; I was always unsure when to be soft and when to be hard, when to call his bluff and when to ignore his latest strop. He was not like

Dolores, a horse that couldn't bear to be fussed, still less bullied. It was in learning Bullseye that I realised how blessed I had been, how absolutely mind-bogglingly lucky I had been, in acquiring Dolores. She was the horse for me, even though I didn't know it. Bullseye, specifically bred to be the horse for me, was nothing of the kind.

I had some difficult times with Bullseye, especially towards the end; some traumatic times, some seriously painful times. I wanted it all to work out. I had invested rather too much emotion in it all. In the end, I had to admit defeat. I was, at bottom, unable to give him enough time: always the problem for someone who tries to combine the horsey life with the arts of earning a living.

Thanks to the recommendation of a friend, Bullseye found a berth at a riding school, where, with his big, handsome looks and his big, handsome paces, he was adored by all the girls who went there. He was given loads of work and loads of attention, and found his niche. The story had a reasonably happy ending, though we had a hard time getting there.

But Bullseye and I had one day of perfection, one day in heaven, and it is with that memory that I will conclude his part of the story. Dolores and Bullseye were then at a new livery yard, a lovely place deep in darkest Suffolk. We had moved the horses there for a year or so because of an expansion in the breeding programme: Cind was pregnant again, and we needed a little freedom of movement. The yard decided to hold a twenty-mile pleasure ride, with way-marked trails, riders timed out and timed back, rosettes for all finishers and a grand day out for all. Bullseye and I set off in the company of Liz and St John. Liz was a groom at the yard, an agreeable and rather dashing girl-about-Suffolk; St John was a horse of much character and bottomless stamina, and was rather a mate of Bullseye's.

It was May. We set off in a gentle, soft rain. And once we got moving, we moved. We alternated mad gallops with hand-on-the-buckle strolls: Bullseye loved it. He was up for everything, and had the day of his life. He galloped as if he would never stop; he walked as if he was the most easy and relaxed horse on the planet. We travelled the soft paths of the Suffolk sandlings, kept cool by the soft rain, walked and talked, rounded a corner, saw another inviting prospect and having been invited, entered in and kicked on. Again.

These events are strictly non-competitive: it is a Caucus-race, of the kind organised by the Dodo in *Alice*, in which you run when you like and leave off when you like and everybody gets a prize. Nevertheless, Bullseye had the fastest time of the day: we finished the course in ten minutes under two hours, vastly at peace with the world and with each other. If only it were always like this.

Tom's view

Most horsey people are looking for some kind of intimacy. This intimacy doubles and trebles when you and the horse are sharing a home. Your entire thinking changes; your entire relationship changes. You fret about small nuances in appetite, microscopic alterations in behaviour, subtle differences of expression. Seasons change and the horse changes with them. In winter, you worry about getting the feed right and keeping condition on the horse; in the warmer months, you worry about too much time on the field and a big wobbly grass-belly. In autumn, you prepare for the months of deprivation; in spring, the air fills with hair as you groom, the coat begins to glow and shine, the eye looks as if its owner is ready for anything.

So it was that spring with Dolores. She had looked a little rough that winter. In February, in early March, she had looked like an old horse, like a retired horse, like a horse that no longer had much purpose. But then spring sprang, and day by day she looked lovelier, a picture of health, a picture of content. It seemed that I was capable of looking after a horse, capable of giving her what she needed, capable of arranging life in a way she enjoyed.

There is a great day in the horsey year, for those of us who keep horses at home. It is Naked Horse Day: the first day the sun has some real heat in it, the first day that you know for sure that winter is dead. And so you turn out your horses without their rugs on: no bulky, muddy, clammy mass of waterproofing and straps. Out they go, the sun on their coats and in their eyes, and all of them shining. They roll on the ground and get all filthy, leaving roll-patches covered with the loose hair they have rubbed off, and then they attend to each other, grooming one another with a joyful frenzy, each reaching for the other the places you can't reach for yourself. It is a celebration of solidarity and friendship: it is a celebration of spring. And Dolores looked, almost from one day to the next, like the most fabulous and healthy young mare.

And the vet came. One of the problems of having horses at home is knowing when to call the vet. It is a test of nerve: it pits concern for the horse against economy. Alas, the concern and the vet always win. I can't remember the nature of the emergency on this historic occasion, though I know it didn't concern Dolores. It was Tom who came by, a rangy red-haired Irishman, a top vet and very decent guy, and he dealt with whatever it was with calm efficiency.

So I asked him to have a look at Dolores. Here's another thing about a vet's visit: if you've got one on the premises, you want him to do as much work as he can and to look at as many horses as possible, all under the cost of a single visit. True, there was nothing wrong with Dolores: au contraire, but I had an impulse. I had a question, and I wanted to have Tom's view. As a vet, as a horseman. He thought she was looking great.

"Sure, she'd bear you another. But put her to something light-boned."

Neptune's daughter

So Dolores went to meet an Anglo-Arab called Heritage Neptune. He was a stunning little horse – light-boned all right – who still competed in the sport of eventing at two-star level, which is pretty amazing for a working stallion. Dolores came back full of foal and slipped happily back into her trance of maternity: round, soft-eyed, eating anything we put in front of her. She was serene and happy and healthy over the long winter, and then as spring returned, she came back into herself: bursting with health and with life. After eleven months, we were ready to rock, but this time, there were no car journeys, no rattling coffee cups, no long-distance care. She was at home, and we could keep an eye on her throughout the day and for that matter, the night. She was in the big box behind the house at night; by day, she was in the front paddock. I would be with her all right. True, I had a pretty difficult schedule, but I got back every single night, got up every two or three hours and checked things out. No foal: only one horse in the box just like before. Inevitably, there was a single night when I couldn't make it back, and inevitably, that's when the foal was born.

Cind went down and checked Dolores at two in the morning, and found her calm, cool-skinned, dry, eating hay. She went down at four and found her in exactly the same state. Cind was turning and about to go back to bed when she realised that there were rather more legs in the box than there had been a couple of hours back. And there, on the far side, was the little foal: bright bay with a white star, and suckling like mad. Cind called me at once: we had a filly-foal.

So we called her Davenport Girl. A moment to explain. Heritage Neptune lived in a part of Suffolk known as the Heritage Coast and naturally, he was named for the sea. Now Cind's mother was brought up along the Suffolk coast. She had lived with her mother and father, in one of the last Thames sailing barges to work the coast for cargo. The boat was the *Davenport*. It was Cind's mother and the family connection that had brought us to Suffolk: and the *Davenport* that had carried Cind's mother for the first seven years of her life. So not a bad name, if a mite personal. Dani for short.

A harem of mares

I have four horses living at home with me. One is a Shetland called Sophie, bought as a companion for the others, for horses hate to be on their own, and can get very silly when left alone. She is a feisty little thing. Eddie, my younger boy, sits on her in the good weather. He rides bareback, though we have to stand around like slip-catchers when he does so, because self-preservation isn't his strongest instinct. Joe used to ride her, but the horsey thing never really got to him; perhaps the horsey gene has skipped a generation. He is now fourteen and six feet tall, so Shetland ponies are no longer an option for him anyway. But Eddie thinks she's great.

There is also Dani, who has trained on to become a lovely little mare: full of spark and personality, with great paces. She has the trustfulness that Bullseye lost, not least because she weaned herself naturally in the company of another mare and foal. I have done most of the work on her myself, with the help and advice of my friend Juliet, a horse-woman of genius. It is invidious to make comparisons, especially to compare people with their parents, but

Dani is a joy to be with.

She is stabled with Rusty, a horse that Cind bought on a wild and glorious whim. Rusty is an Appaloosa-cross-thoroughbred: white and covered with brown spots, outrageously lovely. People stop their cars and gaze when we pass. She is also as kind a mare as you could hope to meet.

And there is Dolores, 30 now in sight, still getting a kick out of life, still with her coat and her eye glowing in the spring, still whickering to greet me in the morning, still striding out beside me when I put her away at night. My home life is structured and punctuated by the needs of horses. When I look from the windows of my house, I can see her out in the meadow, her head down, giving the grass the attention it deserves.

Eddie

Sometimes Eddie helps me to feed the horses. I ask him in words if he wants to do so: I back up the words with Makaton signs. I bring my right hand to my mouth: "Do you want to feed – " and then I place two fingers of my right hand, tips pointing to the floor, astride two fingers of my left hand, held out like a gun "– the horses?"

If he is not too distracted, he will agree, and I will help him with his wellies and we will go and mix the feeds. He is seven now, and quite capable of doing the job: "This is for Sophie... This is for Dolly." "Sophie!" he will say. "Dolly!" And he will mix the chaff, the grain, the sugar beet and the supplements, each as I pass it to him, and stir them all in together. Not terribly well, it must be said, but I stir myself and then ask him to finish the job for me. Eddie, you see, has Down's Syndrome. He is at his happiest among horses and dogs: he is confident and fearless and really quite tact-ful when among them.

So he and I put the bowls of food in the stables, and then Eddie carries a head collar to the field gate. Dolores gives us a whicker of welcome: "See, she's saying hello. Now you wait here one second."

And I attach the head collar, and lead Dolores out of the field and close the gate. Then I give the lead rope to Eddie and vanish. I disappear round to the far side, so that I can guide Dolores by a nudge in the side or a yank of the mane if I need to. But mostly I don't. Dolores understands the situation perfectly: she knows there is a foal-type creature ahead and that she needs to be grown up and responsible and maternal. So Eddie leads her in: a horse twice as tall as he is, walking calmly and generously alongside him. And Eddie is filled with delight, loving to be with these enormous, beautiful and generous creatures. It is where he likes to be. Of all the great things Dolores has done for me in her lifetime, this is the equal of any. At the last moment before the stables, I magically reappear, take the lead rope and walk the final steps into her box. I remove the head collar, and Dolores puts her head in her bowl. I then lift Eddie up so he can see over the door, see that the food he had put together has found favour: a deeply satisfying sight, as I know well.

We complete the job with the other three horses, and then it is time to go back into the house. At the last, we say goodnight to Dolores: Eddie will usually sign his goodnight as well as say it. From her box the sound of munching: she's finished her short feed and now she is eating her hay. A munching horse: it is the very sound of contentment, the perfect music of peace. We've had some times, she and I.

Simon Barnes is the multi-award-winning chief sportswriter for *The Times*. He is also a novelist, nature writer and horseman, and the author of a dozen books, including the bestselling *How to be a Bad Birdwatcher* and *The Meaning of Sport* (Short Books). He lives in Suffolk with his family.